Backyard Rockets

Backyard Rockets

Learn to Make and Launch Rockets, Missiles, Cannons, and Other Projectiles

Instructables.com

Edited by Mike Warren

Skyhorse Publishing

Skyhorse Publishing books may be purchased in bulk at special discounts for sales promotion, corporate gifts, fund-raising, or educational purposes. Special editions can also be created to specifications. For details, contact the Special Sales Department, Skyhorse Publishing, 307 West 36th Street, 11th Floor, New York, NY 10018 or info@skyhorsepublishing.com.

Skyhorse® and Skyhorse Publishing® are registered trademarks of Skyhorse Publishing, Inc.®, a Delaware corporation.

Visit our website at www.skyhorsepublishing.com.

10 9 8 7 6 5 4 3 2 1

Library of Congress Cataloging-in-Publication Data is available on file.

ISBN: 978-1-62087-730-2

Printed in China

Disclaimer:

This book is intended to offer general guidance. It is sold with the understanding that every effort was made to provide the most current and accurate information. However, errors and omissions are still possible. Any use or misuse of the information contained herein is solely the responsibility of the user, and the author and publisher make no warrantees or claims as to the truth or validity of the information. The author and publisher shall have neither liability nor responsibility to any person or entity with respect to any loss or damage caused, or alleged to have been caused, directly or indirectly, by the information contained in this book. Furthermore, this book is not intended to give professional dietary, technical, or medical advice. Please refer to and follow any local laws when using any of the information contained herein, and act responsibly and safely at all times.

Table of Contents

Introduction

The backyard is where all the cool projects happen. Projects where things might start on fire, move at high speed, make loud noises, or otherwise jeopardize the safety of grandma's heirloom crystal collection are some of the most fun builds you can do. But they have to be done outside, and ideally near a first-aid kit. Which is why, for me, the backyard has always been a place where large (and occasionally dangerous) projects get their time to shine.

In *Backyard Rockets*, we celebrate the courage, skill, and ingenuity that comes with firing projectiles into the air without an advanced degree in aeronautical engineering. You don't need to be a rocket scientist to try out any of the DIY rocketry projects in this book, but we won't hold it against you if you are.

Professionals, amateurs, students, and just plain pyromaniacs have all contributed projects to Instructables.com, and we've made this collection of the best rocket projects on the site. You'll find simple projects to get started in your backyard, and we've included a few that you might consider trying a few miles outside of town.

We've curated the projects in this book to get you started with beginner rocket projects like stomp-rockets (page 24), all the way to more complex projects like rockets with an in-flight camera (page 183). Whether you're looking for a low-tech project for a weekend kids birthday party or a big build using all kinds of components, Backyard Rocketry has a project for you.

What are you waiting for? Get making, and transform your quiet yard from a place to relax to a live testing field where rockets can blast off and reach for the sky. No matter what your technical level you're sure to find a fun project here to satiate your rocket appetite, just remember to bring a fire extinguisher in case there's an accident and you need to scrub the launch.

Mike Warren
Editor, Instructables.com

Section 1
Small Rockets

Liquid Fuel Rocket

By: Tool Using Animal
(http://www.instructables.com/
id/Office-Supplies-Challenge-
Liquid-Fuel-Rocket/)

This Instructable demonstrates how to make a Liquid Fuel Rocket from office supplies. Warning, this is kind of dangerous—I had one blow up in my hand already. It was more startling than anything; the two halves flew off in different directions (wear leather gloves just to be safe). They'll fly about 75 feet straight up.

Step 1: You Will Need

- A sharpie
- Canned air
- Electrical tape (substitute packing tape)
- Ballpoint pen
- Rubber band
- Bottle cap
- Leatherman or other pocket knife
- Robot sticker (optional)

Step 2: The Rocket Body

Disassemble the sharpie and remove the ink and the point. Cut a piece of ink tube ¾ inch long from a ballpoint pen and wrap one half with a small piece of electrical tape. Insert the tube into the

sharpie where the point used to be and tap it until firmly seated. Reassemble the two halves of the sharpie.

Step 3: Guidance

The fins are made by folding tape over on itself and attaching the tag ends to the rocket body. Trim into a rocket-ish profile. Attach three equally spaced around the body.

Step 4: Propulsion

Take the canned air, bend the straw down next to the body, space it out with the bottle cap, and secure with a rubber band.

Step 5: Launch

Outside, invert the can of canned air and slip the rocket body onto the straw. Hold the rocket body and depress the trigger on the can, allow a short time to pass, and release the rocket. Wash, rinse, repeat.

3

A Rocket in Your Pocket

By: Kiteman
(http://www.instructables.com/
id/A-Rocket-in-your-Pocket/)

Not just a rocket in your pocket, but an entire rocket factory and launch system!

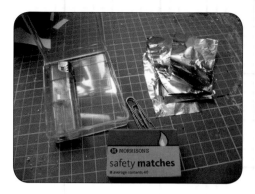

Step 1: Materials

The materials are easy to find in most modern homes:
- A pocket-sized box
- A box of matches
- A small scrap of wood
- Some pieces of kitchen foil
- Optional extra: a pocket lighter.

Step 2: Making the Launch Pad

Take the scrap of wood and trim it to fit inside the box. Halfway along it, drill a small hole at an angle of 45°—the hole needs to be just large enough to fit a matchstick into.

4

Step 3: Outfitting the Kit

Er, well, you just put it all in the box. . . . If you put the pieces of foil at the bottom, they'll stay flatter.

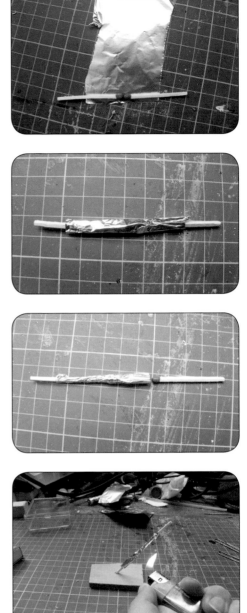

Step 4: Making and Launching a Rocket

Take one piece of foil and lay two matches head-to-head at one end. Roll the matches up in the foil. Make sure that one match can slide out of the foil tube you've made, though not too easily. Twist the foil tightly around the other match. Slot the rocket into the launcher and apply heat to the middle of the foil, either with another match or with the lighter. After a few moments, the heat conducted by the foil will light the match-heads, and . . . *woosh!* . . . off it will go.

I could make a lot of fuss about health and safety, but if you're old enough to be allowed to play with matches, you're old enough to know where and when you should launch rockets like this. If you set fire to the cat and burn down the garden, it's your own fault.

Teeny, Tiny Rocket Engine

By: Adam Kelly
(killerjackalope)
(http://www.instructables.com/
id/Teeny-tiny-rocket-engine/)

"Adam you never cease to make me feel like my brain is about to fall out my ears lol you're never just like reading a book"

That is a text I received after telling Sammi what I did today. This is what I did today.

I am unsure why I did this or what purpose, if any, it could serve. It does propel itself in a direction, though it more or less explodes forward. It went straight across, hit the counter, leaving a small mark, and then went back in to the depths of the kitchen. It may have surprised my housemate a little—probably should have told him why he was lighting my match . . .

First issue, propellant? I reckon Swan matches; they're pretty bad because they light slower than most. Seems like it's about the right mix of burn-y but not explode-y . . .

Wait, what will I use as the body? More to the point, where did this idea even come from if the propellant was the first question? This is some kind of bizarre causation loop in my head.

Anyway, I realized an earring back might work, as the end of the casing is about the size I'd expect for the nozzle. (I did no science here, I just decided this.) I didn't figure out the capping of the other end until later.

Anyway . . .

Oh, stop. This is dangerous. Grinding up matches is a logically foolish activity that may lead to burns.Bbreak up small amounts at a time to keep it from surprising you and burning your hand. Lighting this thing might go badly. Cover your eyes and remember that constructing it may be a danger—take care.

Step 1: Tools and Materials

Tools
- Pliers
- A knife
- A card
- A hard surface

Materials
- Matches (keep the box handy too)
- An earring back (clutch back that is; see photos)

Step 2: Prepare the Casing

Remove the end cap of the earring back. Remove the inner plastic clutch (this still works as a back). To remove it, get a drawing pin or nail and push it into the inner hole, then pull it out. The object just needs to be thicker than the earring pins that went through it before.

Step 3: Prepare the Match-Head Propellant

This is relatively simple, but inherently dangerous with strike-anywhere matches. No metal on metal or stone on stone. I used an upended ashtray (glass) and chopped the stuff up as well as I could with a knife. Next, I used my old tech card to finely chop it repeatedly. This worked nicely. The technique is the same as you might use with certain illicit substances, but slightly rougher. It doesn't need to be powdered, just fairly fine, like granulated sugar.

Step 4: Loading the Powder

Poke a hole in the match box and press the empty casing in to it— it'll hold it until it's nearly finished. I used a scalpel as a teeny little spade. Carefully fill the casing; start with a few lumps to stop the finer stuff falling out the bottom. As you go, use the end of match (not the head) to stamp it down. By the end, you want it to be thoroughly packed in, essentially solid. Leave at least a millimeter between the end and the powder.

Step 5: Cut Capping Piece

This doesn't entirely cap the thing; it's just there to help with sealing the end. Cut a small rough circle that drops in on top of the propellant; it should pretty much fill the end over.

small

7

Step 6: Seal the End

To seal the end, fold the rim over inwards with pliers. Now carefully squeeze the lip flat. Bend it over a little and squeeze again. Repeat this a few times. You'll need to squeeze hard to seal it up. By the end, it should look like a single piece of metal. I wouldn't do this in a vice unless it's small and fairly easy to be accurate with.

Step 7: Launch It

I bent a beer can's pull ring in to a stand for firing the rocket . . . then lit it . . .

Ten-Minute Rocket

By: (zack)
(http://www.instructables.com/
id/10-Minute-Rocket/)

This Instructable will teach you how to build a simple, ultra-light rocket from household items (and of course a rocket engine). Here's the supply list:

- 1 tube of superglue
- 1 roll of tinfoil
- 1 straw big enough to fit around your launch rod
- 1 deck of playing cards that you don't mind parting with
- 1 C rocket engine
- Several rocket engine detonators and plugs
- 1 electronic detonator (and necessary cables)

WARNING: This is totally dangerous. I didn't die, but you might. It is *not my fault* if you hurt yourself following these instructions.

Step 1: Building Yourself Some Fins

The fins themselves are pretty simple: the difficult part is positioning them evenly around the rocket. To make a fin, first you'll need to fold a playing card in half hamburger style. Take your superglue

and seal the folded halves together, like a sandwich. Glue is going to ooze out the sides and get all over your fingers Suck it up and take it like a man. Make two of these sandwiches and let the glue completely dry. Now you need to do a little bit of measuring, but nothing too complicated. Take one of the folded cards and put it perpendicular to the other, forming an L. Mark off the edge and cut it away so you're left with one square-ish shape. Repeat with the other folded card and, if you've done everything correctly thus far, you should be left with two pseudo-squares. Take these faux-squares and cut diagonally across from the curved corner to the corner directly opposite. You should now have four fin shapes, congratulations. Now onto the difficult part: attaching them.

Step 2: Attaching the Fins

Basically, you want the fins to be completely perpendicular to each other. I realize that this is darn near impossible; but if you somehow screw up the positioning horribly, the rocket could possibly come back and hit you in the face. Take your time. I've attached a template PDF to the end of this Instructable; I would recommend printing it out and using it as a guide when you're gluing. Superglue is really *really* good at bonding cardboard, so you're only going to get one shot at this. Line up your engine, apply a small amount of glue to the edge of the fin, and take the dive. The first fin is the easiest, but every other fin has to be positioned as accurately as possible to prevent the rocket from spinning out. Again, just take your time and it should be fine. Once you have all the fins loosely attached, apply a liberal amount of glue to the seams. You do not want one of these falling off mid flight. Put the rocket in the sun to dry; the next step is going to take a while.

Step 3: Sculpting a Nose Cone

Take a large piece of aluminum foil, about 5" by 5", and begin to shape it into a cone. This step is a little tricky and takes a bit of practice, but you'll probably get it after your third or fourth failed cone. You'll want to rub it on a smooth surface to work out all the kinks, and over time (with liberal amounts of elbow grease) the cone should begin to take shape. Be sure to check that the tip is centered after every few minutes of honing; if it is skewed it could also affect the trajectory of your rocket. Once you're satisfied with your cone, just glue it onto the end of your rocket. Mine happened to fit perfectly within the cardboard tube, but it's fine if yours is a bit larger. I applied a good puddle of glue around the cone and waited for it to harden, just to ensure the cone was attached snugly.

Step 4: Attaching the Launch Lug

Cut a piece of straw about the length of your rocket's body. Carefully glue it between two of your fins, and position it parallel to the body. Wait for it to dry, and then again apply more glue. You don't want this one to fall off either: it's a pretty crucial part of the rocket. Once your launch lug is dried on, you're all done. Find a good open area to launch it and prepare the detonator.

Step 5: LAUNCH

Carefully insert the detonator and seal the hole with a plug. Clip the leads onto the ends of the detonator and tilt the launch pad away from you at about a 45° angle. Step back, and press the button. If all goes according to plan, the rocket should shoot off the launch pad and fly pretty darn far.

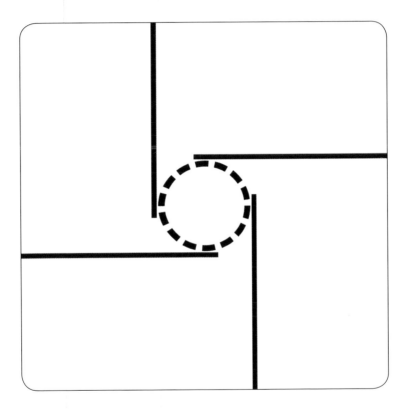

Ultimate Straw Rocket
By: pudi.dk
(http://www.instructables.com/
id/Ultimate-Straw-Rocket!/)

What is the Ultimate Straw Rocket? Answer: A very easy-to-make rocket, made from a drinking straw and launched using air pressure. Almost everyone will be able to make this; it does not require any hard-to-find items. It also can be made in very little time. Therefore the rockets themselves will be very easy to mass produce. They will fly *high* up in the air and then land on the ground, completely safe! Okay, let's get started!

Step 1: Gathering Materials
As first said, the items are very easy to get, and you probably already have them lying around your house. At the end of this Instructable are cutouts needed for this rocket.
- (Colorful) straws
- Hot glue gun
- Pair of scissors
- A bike pump
- The printed document

Step 2: Making the Rocket
Cut a 6 cm piece of a straw. Put a dot of hot glue in one end of the straw, making sure it's air tight.

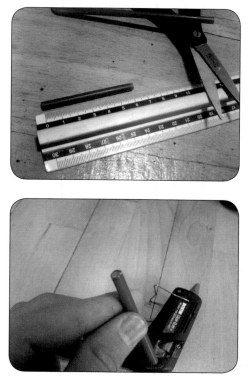

Step 3: Attaching Fins
Now cut out a pair of fins from the printed document. Then fold and glue the fins together. Stippled lines mean "fold backwards," whereas straight lines mean the opposite. You can use hot glue

to glue the fins together, but I find that white glue (Elmer's glue or wood glue) works well. Then glue the backside (the white side) and attach it around the straw, approximately 1–1.5 cm from the open end of the straw.

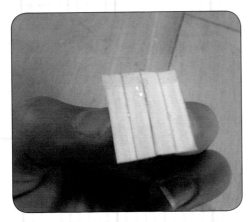

Step 4: Launch It!

The rocket is finished now! Wasn't that easy? Now for launching it: Insert it all the way down in the nozzle of the bike pump, and give the bike pump a good, fast pump! Now enjoy your small flying rockets. I had my rockets to go as high as ~10 meters! Don't forget goggles: you don't want the rocket in your, or everyone else's, eyes. Thanks to Peter Hald for inspiration.

small

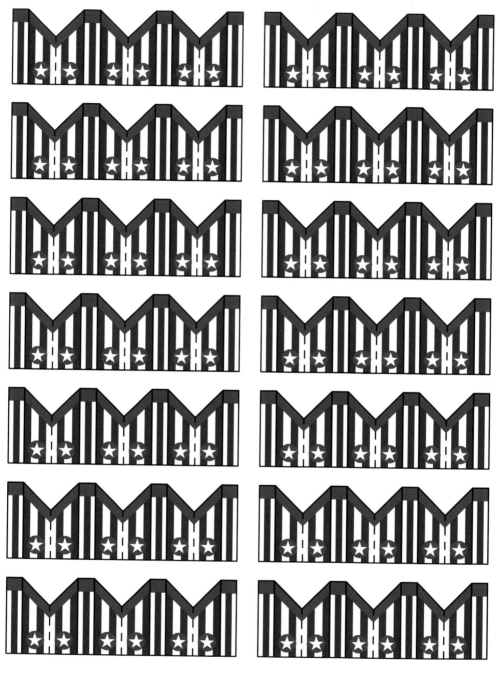

Ultimate Straw Rocket
- by Bunjabin

You can use a copier to scale these fin designs up or down as needed.

Section 2
Air-Powered Rockets

Compressed Air Rockets

By: Mike Warren
(mikeasaurus)
(http://www.instructables.com/
id/compressed-air-rockets/)

When I was at the Bay Area Maker Faire earlier this year, I saw a display that had a compressed air paper rocket launcher. Kids would make their own paper rockets, load them onto a launching tube, and fire them into the sky. I thought it was pretty cool, but I wanted something more ~~dangerous~~ different.

So, how do you make compressed air rockets better? By making exploding compressed air paper rockets!

Using simple Chinatown fireworks, combined with an elastic deployment system to eject a small toy parachute action figure, I designed a rocket that jettisons the parachute man from altitude. I made three test rockets, which were designed to test and calibrate the compressed air launcher and six live rockets, which were intended to test the theory and intent of my design. Unfortunately, it didn't quite turn out the way it was supposed to. All six live rockets exploded, melted, or malfunctioned and no parachute men were successfully deployed.

So, instead of this being a how-to, it's more of a how-not-to.

Obviously working with fireworks, compressed air, power tools, and rockets is dangerous business. Use common sense and work within your ability.

Enough talk: let's explode some rockets!

Step 1: Tools and Materials
Tools
- Hacksaw
- Wood saw
- Drill and bits (various sizes, wood bits)
- Scissors
- Hobby knife
- PVC glue
- Lighter
- Masking tape
- Bicycle pump

Materials
- PVC pipe
- 1 × 2" diameter pipe (roughly 24" long)
- 1 × 2" cap
- 1 × 2" diameter to 1.5" diameter bushing
- 2 × 1" threaded coupler
- 1 × 1" diameter pipe (roughly 24" long)
- Launch platform
- Scrap wood uprights
- Scrap ¼" plywood base
- Scrap 2" × 4" for blocking
- Scrap 2" × 4" for launcher stabilizer
- Sprinkler valve (1" ingress/egress)
- Compressed air-gun trigger
- Schrader valve (inner tube valve)
- Paper

- Cardboard/card stock
- Elastic bands
- Threaded rod and wingnut
- Cable ties

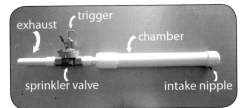

Step 2: Launcher—Overview

All compressed air rocket launchers work under the principle of rapidly displacing air to launch a projectile. Air can be pressurized in a chamber and then deployed by means of a trigger or stored in a bladder and squeezed to be released. These are active and passive systems.

Active or pressurized assemblies are capable of producing some spectacular results due to the high pressure able to be stored in the chamber. Passive systems like stomp rockets reply on the pressure created when the air bladder is squeezed. This project focuses on the former.

The setup of this pressurized air launcher is simple:

- Air is supplied through a bicycle pump attached to the intake nipple.
- Air is held in the pressure chamber until it is released by the trigger.
- The trigger is attached to a modified sprinkler valve (pilot valve).
- When the trigger is activated, air is released through the exhaust.

Keen observers of Instructables.com may recognize this canon as Fungus Amungus' Christmas canon. This is the same canon but adapted to fit on a launching pad. And this version shoots exploding rockets—not confetti.

Step 3: Launcher—Detail

Chamber

This canon was made with about 28" of 2" PVC pipe as the chamber. Cut your 2" pipe to length and glue on the 2" cap to one of the ends. On the other end, glue on the 2" to 1" bushing. Then, cut a 4–6" length of 1" PVC and glue that into the bushing. Finally, glue the 1" threaded coupler onto the 1" pipe attached to the bushing. Set chamber assembly aside for 24 hours until glue has cured. Once set, drill an opening in the cap for the Schrader valve. Tap the opening and wrap the valve in Teflon tape and screw it into the opening.

Sprinkler Valve

I did not perform the modifications to this valve. It appears that the valve has had the electronic solenoid removed and replaced with the handle and trigger for a compressed air nozzle. The trigger is threaded and fits directly into the place where the solenoid trigger was. Replacing the electronic portion was a simple mechanical action. The valve is 1" female threaded on both ends.

Exhaust

Cut a length of 12" to 14" of 1" PVC pipe, then glue the threaded couple to one end. Set aside to dry.

air

19

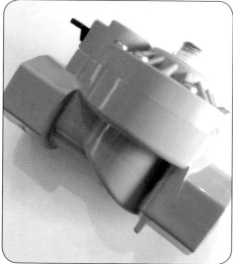

layers of masking tape. The masking tape allows the rocket to withstand the pressure when the PVC pipe is filled with air, and the card stock provides a rigid flat base for the rest of the payload to be built upon.

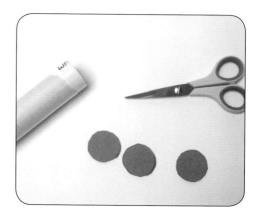

Step 4: Rocket Assembly— Fuselage

Time to make our rockets! Take an A4 (8.5" × 11") sheet of paper and roll it lengthwise, using a 1" PVC pipe as our frame. When the paper has been completely rolled tape the length with masking tape.

Next, cover the top of the paper with a cardboard or card stock circle roughly the same size as the pipe (1" diameter). Then secure it in place using several

Step 5: Rocket Assembly— Payload

The payload is the trickiest part of the assembly, and errors here are probably what brought my project to failure.

Lower Assembly (Charge)

After the fuselage was completed, a short cylinder of card stock was installed on top of the bottom deck previously installed. The cylinder was secured with plenty of masking tape, and a firework was installed inside. Notches were made in two places on the top portion of the cylinder after its installation: one at the location where the firework will explode/emit flame and another off to the side, which will allow the fuse to pass through and be lit once the assembly is closed.

With the firework installed, another circle of card stock was covered in aluminum foil and installed over the cylinder opening. More masking tape was used to secure the charge in place, ensuring that the notched openings created earlier weren't covered.

Upper Assembly (Parachute Man)

Another longer card stock cylinder was made and attached to the lower assembly in just one small area using masking tape, making the top cylinder hinged. This hinge will allow the payload to open when ignited and the brave parachute soldier will be deployed. Well, that was the idea. The top of the upper assembly was capped with another circle of card stock, then a parachute soldier was inserted into the assembly. Close the upper assembly and use a single strip of masking tape over the notch made earlier for the firework explosion point. A cone of paper was added to the top after the payload was finished.

Elastic Mechanism

To allow the upper assembly to flap open when the masking tape strap was severed, an elastic was used. Cut a rubber band and fix one end to the upper assembly, pull taught, and fix the other end to the base of the fuselage. I used masking tape to secure the elastic in place.

Step 6: Launch Platform

Since I was going to be filming, lighting fireworks, and pulling the compressed air trigger, I needed a platform to hold the launcher. I made this launch platform in less than an hour with scrap wood hanging around the shop. This platform is made from a 12" × 12" × ½" sheet of plywood, a drawer face that measured 6" × 48" × ½", and some 2" × 4" off-cuts of various lengths.

A threaded rod was installed near the top and through a 2" × 4", which allows the launcher to be directed at an angle. You know, in case I wanted to launch exploding rockets at the neighbors and not just straight up. Holes were drilled into the top movable

air

platform, which the launcher will be strapped to with cable ties.

could be damaged, and this should be definitely be undertaken by someone who knows what they are doing. Not heeding my own advice, I launched from the roof of the Instructables.com lab in downtown San Francisco.

Here's a few images from rockets 1–3 shown from different angles.

rocket #1

rocket #2

Step 7: Launch!

With the assembly done, it's time to test the rockets out. You should probably launch someplace that is wide-open and has no people or buildings nearby that

rocket #3

Step 8: Results

My measure of success for this project was successful deployment of the parachute soldier at altitude. To that end, this project did not work as intended. However, it was loads of fun to make, and any project I can walk away from with all my fingers should be seen as a positive learning experience.

That's it, get outside and fire off some rockets. Be safe and have fun!

pilot from rocket #6

rocket #5
ignited in flight

rocket #4
opened, didn't eject

rocket #6
ignited in flight

air

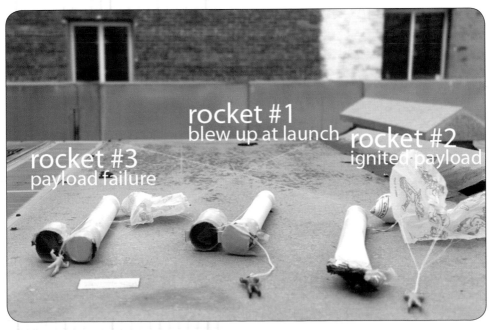

rocket #1
blew up at launch

rocket #2
ignited payload

rocket #3
payload failure

Paper Stomp Rockets

By: seamster
(http://www.instructables.com/
id/Paper-Stomp-Rockets-Easy-
and-Fun/)

I run a free summertime activity program for kids as part of my job in the city where I live. So I've got a lot of fun little projects up my sleeves, and I'm always on the lookout for more. One of the more popular summertime activities in my repertoire is homemade stomp rockets. Stomp rockets are great because they are both creative and physical.

There are many versions of paper stomp rockets and launchers out there. They all work essentially the same way: Air is forced through a PVC contraption, which launches a lightweight paper rocket up into the air. This particular launcher design is a combination of a handful of ideas I've seen, along with a few of my own additions.

I have a basic rocket design that I drew up that uses a single sheet of paper, which I've included as a PDF at the end of this Instructable.

Read on, and then go have some fun.

Step 1: Materials

This launcher design produces no waste, and should cost around $10.

For One Launcher
- One 10' length of ½" PVC
- One ½" 90° elbow (all fittings are of the slip variety)
- One ½" four-way fitting
- Two ½" end caps
- One 1" coupling
- One 1" × ½" bushing
- One 2-liter soda bottle cap
- Lots of 2-liter soda bottles

Other Necessary Supplies
- PVC cement
- Hot glue
- White glue
- Cotton balls
- Tape
- Sheets of 8.5" × 11" paper
- Lots of copies of the attached PDF rocket template

Step 2: Cut the PVC

From your 10' length of PVC, cut the following pieces:

- One 40" piece
- One 18" piece
- One 5" piece
- Two 12" pieces
- Three 11" pieces

Of all the pieces to be cut, accuracy is the most crucial on the three 11" pieces. These will be made into forming tubes, which will be used to help make the actual rockets. Construction of the forming tubes is covered in Step 5.

Step 3: Build Basic Launcher Assembly

The photos should provide enough detail on how to construct the basic launcher assembly. Use PVC cement to put it all together.

The 12" pieces are the side supports that make the base. The 18" piece is the riser from which the rockets will launch. I used my palm sander to quickly knock off the sharp edge of the launch-end of the 18" piece of PVC.

The 1" coupling and the 1" × ½" bushing go together to make the bottle end of the launcher.

Step 4: Make the Bottle End of the Launcher

Two-liter bottles make great bladders for stomp rocket launchers because they're readily available and they're pretty durable. This set-up is especially nice because it allows you to quickly replace bottles when they've been completely worn out or cracked.

Begin by drilling a hole through a 2-liter bottle cap. This is easiest to do while the cap is screwed onto an old bottle.

I prefer to use hot glue to glue the bottle cap into the opening of the 1" coupling. Hot glue is quick, fills the gap between the bottle cap and coupling nicely, and is only semi-permanent.

When the bottle cap itself begins to wear out and the threads are stripped, you can just grab it with a pair of pliers and yank it out to replace it with a new one.

Step 5: Make Rocket Forming Tubes

The three 11" pieces of PVC will be used to make three separate rocket forming tubes. These will help you make perfect rockets every time. It's nice to have a few on hand so more than one person can be working on a rocket at the same time.

You want the forming tubes to be slightly bigger than the tube that the rockets get launched from. This is accomplished by gluing a sheet of 8.5" × 11" paper around each forming tube. I used white glue and glued each sheet directly to the tube, and then to itself after rolling it on tightly.

A piece of tape (I used electrical tape) was wrapped around one end of each paper-covered tube. This is to aid in the construction of the rocket, as detailed in the next step.

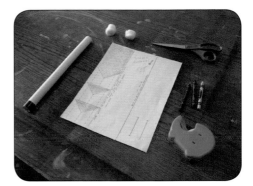

Step 6: Make Some Rockets

Print out and make plenty of copies of the attached PDF rocket template. There are basic building instructions on the rocket template. Decorate and cut out areas as directed.

Roll the rocket body section onto a forming tube, with the bottom of rocket (where the fin placement lines are located) just above the tape at the end of the forming tube. This creates an open space at the top of the tube where the cotton balls will go.

Tape the body tube together, but *not* to the forming tube. Fold the fins and tape them in place on the fin placement lines. Place two cotton balls into the open area at the top of the paper tube, and cover with a couple of pieces of tape. Remove the rocket from forming tube.

27

I have made a total of six launchers, a couple of which were made with 45° angled risers. These have been especially fun.

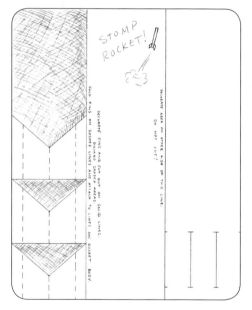

Step 7: Launch!

Before you launch your rockets, be sure to explain some safety rules to everyone involved so nobody gets shot in the eye.

After each launch, you will have to refill the bottle with air. I tell the kids to hold the top of the launch tube with their hand and blow through their hand to fill up the bottle. This way, germ-passing is somewhat minimized.

Vacuum-Cleaner Bazooka

By: ynze
(http://www.instructables.com/
id/Make-a-Vacuum-cleaner-
Bazooka/)

In five minutes, you can build an air-powered bazooka. The bazooka launches plastic capsules about 100 feet. And with some tweaking, you might stretch that distance quite a bit.

Step 1: Stuff You Need

- A vacuum cleaner (any model will do)
- Straight piece of PVC tube, at least 1 meter long with a 35 mm inner diameter. Longer is better (see the text on tweaking)!
- A PVC three-way junction with an angle of 45° that fits the straight PVC tube.
- Duct tape
- A projectile: I used the plastic capsule that is inside "surprise-eggs" (see picture). Old school film

containers work as well. Whatever you use, make sure that the projectile's diameter is just a little smaller than the PVC tubes'.
- A small piece of cardboard (business cards are perfect).

Step 2: Make It

Attach the three-way junction to the straight tube using duct tape (you can glue the parts with PVC glue, of course, but there's no good reason to do so). Wrap duct tape around the tip of the vacuum cleaners' hose, so that it fits snugly into the slanting tube. This fit should be as air-tight as possible. Push the vacuum-cleaners' hose into the slanting tube of the PVC junction

air

part. Test whether the projectile can run smoothly through the assembled PVC tubes when the vacuum-cleaner is attached.

Step 3: Launch It and Tweak It

Launch It

Power up the vacuum cleaner. Cover the tubes' ending with the PVC-junction with the business card. The vacuum cleaner will now suck air from the other end of the PVC tube. Hold the projectile firmly, and insert it in the air-sucking tip of the PVC tube. Let go and enjoy!

Tweak It

If you extend the straight PVC tube, the projectile will be accelerated over a longer period. And so the projectile's velocity will increase. So extend that piece of tube! Add some weight to the projectile. We filled the capsule with rice, but sand might work better. Experiment to find the right weight for the projectile. Again: Have fun! Also, be careful and don't shoot in the direction of living creatures.

Section 3
Soda Bottle Rockets

Fifty-Foot Rubber Band Rocket

By: yokozuna
(http://www.instructables.
com/id/50-Foot-Rubber-Band-
Rocket/)

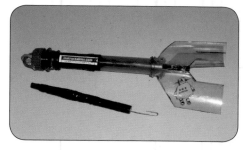

This rocket is based on a kid's toy I saw a couple of years ago that was pretty amazing for the materials involved. I decided to recreate it and see how well my version would work. It was a little heavier than the Styrofoam toy that I had played with, but still seemed to work a lot better than you might expect. And, while you may have a rubber band big enough to reach low earth orbits, I haven't really done anything as far as heat shielding. If you have kids that aren't quite old enough for model rockets, this is the perfect project for them.

I put the original version together in about a half an hour, and played with it for way too long to admit. Eventually it got tore up, and now I've decided to create a new and improved version. This new version boasts some new features, almost all of which are designed to add distance. Starting at the nose cone, it now allows for retractable rubber bands. This will also allow multiple rubber bands to be used where it created too much instability in the original design. The new body is a bit longer, and I figured out a way to help trim down it's circumference a bit and keep it rounder than before. The tail fins are also much larger now to create more spin and, ultimately, more stability. Finally, I now also have a tool to launch the rocket with to avoid accidently thumping your finger on occasion.

Step 1: Build the Nose Cone
Materials
- two 2-liter soda bottles
- 20 oz soda bottle
- Some paperclips
- Rubber bands

Tools
- Hot glue gun
- Pair of scissors
- Needle-nose pliers
- A saw

To get started, we'll begin with the nose cone. Cut off the neck of the bottle, leaving as much of the straight section in place as possible. Next, unscrew the cap and drill a couple of small holes (the size of the paperclip) near the top on two sides. I didn't have a drill handy, and used a small leather punch in place of the drill for now. First, remove and save (without destroying) the sealing ring, then go ahead and put the paperclip in place and screw the lid down tightly. Then you can mark the raised section of the neck for two more holes to keep the paperclip in place. Unscrew the cap and make your holes. Finally, make a hole large enough on top of the cap for at least a couple of rubber bands to fit through.

Now it's time to put it all together. Take the paperclip out and put the rubber band(s) on. The strength, quality, and number of rubber bands you use will make quite a difference on how the rocket performs. This design is a little heavier than the original and needs a little bit more power to fly well. The paperclip on the inside keeps them from falling down into the rocket later on, and you'll be able to dig them out with the launcher (built in the next step) if needed. I placed a golf tee under them so they wouldn't fall back through. I had to use a pair of needle-nose pliers to get the paperclips forced through the holes further down the neck, but that will keep it from falling out. If you need to replace the rubber bands later, it's probably just best to also replace that paperclip.

soda bottle

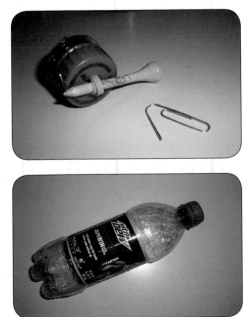

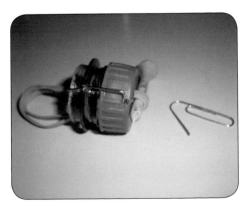

soda bottle

Step 2: Build the Launching Tool

This is the easiest piece to build, and it will help you when you're building the body in the next step. Leave the smaller hook in the paperclip, and straighten out the rest. Take the ballpoint and cap off the pen, leaving the outer hull. Put the paperclip on the fat end, and tape it with the hook facing towards the middle using your favorite type of tape.

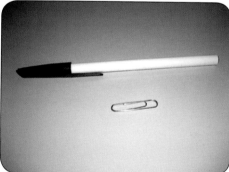

Step 3: The Rocket Body

This is the most difficult step for the build. Strip the labels off the 2-liter bottles, and mark a vertical line on both with a ruler and a sharpie, next to where the label was glued on. Cut around (and keep for now) the top of both bottles, but make sure to leave a little bit of the curve around the entire way. Cut down the vertical line you marked on both bottles, and cut the bottom off around the line where the bottle no longer stays flat. Set one of them aside; that will be for the fins in the next step.

You will probably want to wrap your plastic shell around something roughly the same size as what you want the finished product to be. Wrap it around twice and make sure it is tight and even on both ends; then mark the ends with the sharpie where it meets inside the first layer. Then use the ruler to make a straight line, subtract a little bit to compensate for the PVC (what I wrapped mine around), and cut out the body. Next, I used a spray adhesive on the inside of the bottle and quickly wrapped it back into a roll where it was doubled over again. At this point grab the 2-liter bottle tops you cut off and use them to place over the body to hold it in place at the correct size.

Now that it's drying, you can start working on the hook that will go inside the body. Unfold a paperclip and double it over, as shown in the pictures. A little ways down, you can bend the legs back out at about a 45° angle. Your glue should be drying by now, so figure out how low in the body you need the hook to be and mark the rocket again. I used a hot glue gun to really hold down the outer joint from separating. From there, you can figure out where to drill two small holes for the paperclips to come out the side of the rocket. Use a pair of needle-nose pliers to place it inside—think of it as working on a ship in a bottle. When you finally get it, place the hook in the middle and bend the paperclip down the sides. I then dropped in some hot glue and used a pinky finger to kind of smear where I wanted it to go. Just be careful not to burn yourself.

I used a bit of electrical tape to hold the paperclip to the sides. One last thing to do: I sawed off a couple of rings from each of the bottle lips and placed these near the ends of the rocket body (unglued). They can butt up to the fins and nose cone later, their main purpose is to keep the rocket body round instead of the oblong shape this design tries to force it to be.

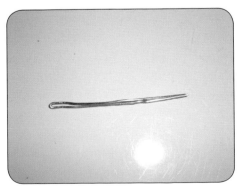

37

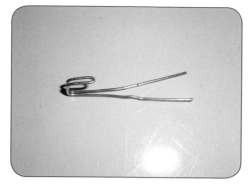

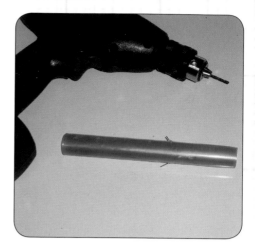

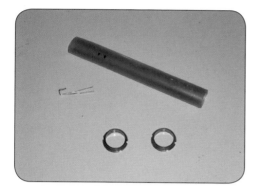

Step 4: Making the Fins

The fins are, what I believe to be, the single most important component in relation to how well it will fly. I flared the ends just a bit (½" up, and 1.5" long). I then angled it out at 45°. The outside of the fin is 2" out and runs up 2.5". Then it also angles out at 45°. The rest is just a small runner to help hold the fins together. I cut out one side of a cocktail straw and placed it over the edge of all three and glued them in place. I then glued the three straws together, being careful to try and keep them all at even distances and angles. A good test on how good the fins are is to try to stand it up when the glue is dry. The straighter it is, the better job you have done. If it is crooked, look it over carefully to see why. A little trimming with a pair of scissors might help fix the problem.

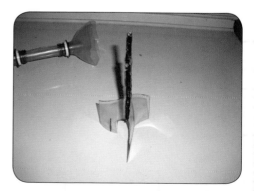

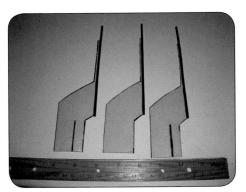

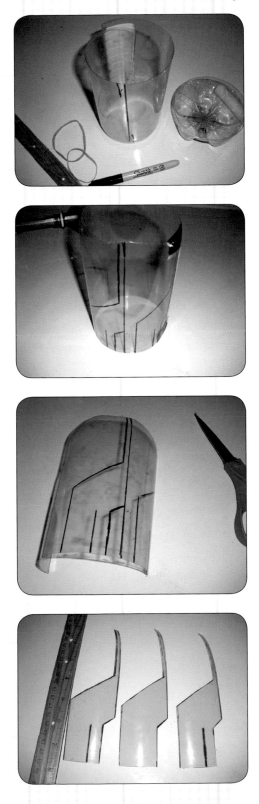

Step 5: Put It All Together

You have the pieces all ready to assemble now. I started with the fins and the body. The side with the slightly rounded top will go up into the nose cone, and the other end will attach to the fins. The hook inside the body will also reflect this. I placed the two together, and, using the sharpie, matched up where they met each other. Slide the lip ring up a little, and use a pair of tin snips to make ½" cut at each mark. This allows the fins to actually go a little ways further up in the body of the rocket, and you can glue them together easier, making it much stronger. Be conservative with the glue on the outside of the rocket, and plaster it in more on the inside for better aerodynamics.

Next, holding the nose cone just off to the side of the top, use your launcher to place the other end of the rubber bands over the hook on the inside. Once they are in place, slide the nose cone as far down onto the rocket as it will go, and slide the other plastic lip up to meet it. I left my hook up a little too high in the rocket, so I also cut the sealing ring we saved from before in half and used that to make a small half moon under the top of the rubber bands. This isn't necessary, but I think it adds to the look and helps keep the rubber bands from being so loose. They don't have to be stretched, but you don't want too much room left over or they may not retract

39

properly. Another problem is that they may become unhooked inside the rocket.

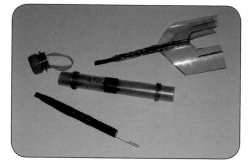

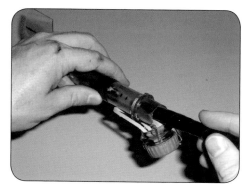

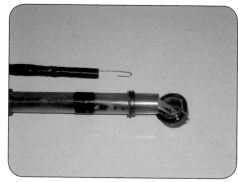

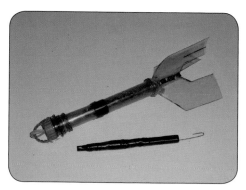

Step 6: Add Some Decals

Now that the rocket itself is finished, you may want to paint it or add decals. I took a robot sticker and cut out both the name and the robot. I put some black electric tape around for a background, then placed the Instructables.com II sticker over this, and put the robot on one of the fins. It gives it a bit more of the feel of a rocket. I also figured out this fits nicely on the end of CD trays, so I might create a "launch pad" display for it when I'm not playing with it. Be warned that, if you create one of these, they are very addictive.

This has been a rebuild of my fifth Instructable, and still one of my favorites. It was a winner in the rubber band contest. I hope the new directions allow you to build one that will fly even further than before. My original "Fifty-Foot Rubber Band Rocket" eventually got up to 78' with some modifications, and I'm hoping this new version can make it up to 100' or more before I'm done with it. The only way to find out . . . build your own and start testing!

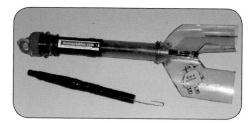

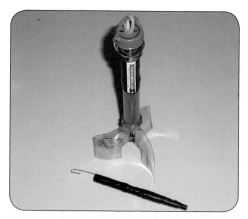

Step 7: Observations of the New Design

I finally got to take a few test shots of the new design. The first thing that I noticed was that my tree has grown a fair amount since the last tests, it was kind of in the way now of where I thought I needed to shoot.

- Shot one: trying to go through tree.
- Shot two: Ttrying to go under tree.
- Shot three: trying to go around tree.
- Shot four: accidently figuring out I can easily go over the tree instead of through it.
- Shot five: over the tree, estimated at 78'. The front edge of the road is 54' from my doorway, the road is 18' across, and it was 5' past the far edge of the road.

The first thing to mention is that, while the sealing ring adds a nice look to the finished rocket, it doesn't stand up very well to the crash landings. After reattaching it a couple of times, I finally gave up and just tore it off. The only other modification I made was the hook on the inside. After having problems trying to catch the rubber bands on it, I realized it was easier to just run a paperclip straight through, catching the rubber bands, and bending it back up the sides of the rocket to hold. I then used some electrical tape to secure and hide the ends of the paperclip.

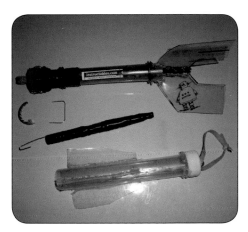

Gasoline-Powered Soda Bottle Rocket Launcher

By: TheGodsMustBeCrazy78
(http://www.instructables
.com/id/Gasoline-Powered-
Soda-Bottle-Rocket-
Launcher.-Desi/)

This Instructable was designed and tested by C. L. Raub.

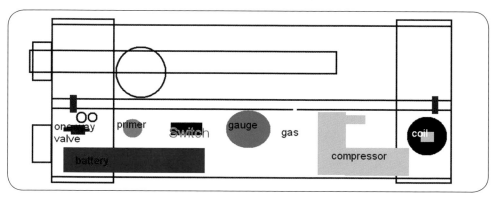

one way valve — primer — Switch — gauge — gas — coil — compressor — battery

Chart 1

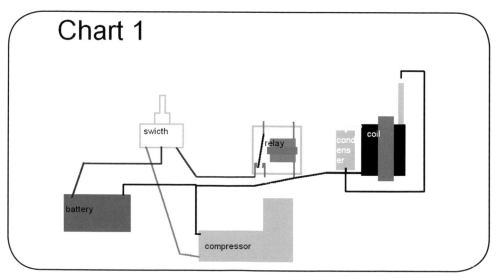

swicth — relay — condenser — coil — battery — compressor

Chart 2

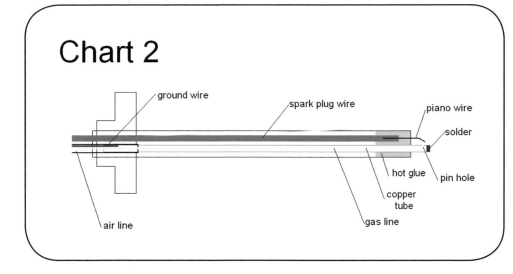

ground wire · spark plug wire · piano wire · solder · hot glue · pin hole · copper tube · gas line · air line

Step 1: What You Need

- 2 3" PVC pipe 15" long
- 3 3" PVC clean outs with caps
- 1 ½" × 12" long plastic threaded pipe
- 1 3" PVC pipe cap
- 1 3" PVC pipe coupler
- 1 2" PVC 90° pipe elbow
- 1 14" piece of ¼" copper tubing
- 1 primer bulb
- 1 on/off momentary switch (or off/on momentary if you use a piezo igniter)
- 1 coil, condenser, relay, or piezo igniter
- 1 12 volt portable air compressor
- 1 can PVC glue
- 1 roll solder
- 1 small tank for gas, ½ to 2 oz
- 1 small one way valve
- 1 pressure gauge, minimum 50 PSI (air pump may include gauge and air T)
- 1 air T
- 1 4' tubing ⅜" OD ¼" ID for air
- 1 4' small gas tubing that will fit in the big tubing (the smaller the better)
- 1 4' spark plug wire
- 1 7.2 to 12 volt stick pack battery, available at hobby shops

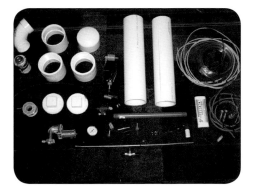

Step 2: Introduction to Assembly

You will need various other parts:

- Super glue
- Wire
- Battery connectors
- Nuts and bolts

If you decide to build this project, you may need to improvise on various parts and construction. All the parts I used may not be available to you, or you may have a better idea about how to construct this project. Either way, you need some building skills and good old fashioned rigging. Good luck.

WARNING: This project has the potential to be dangerous, as you will be igniting compressed gasoline vapor

soda bottle

and using a high voltage coil, which could result in shock. If you make this gas-powered soda bottle rocket, please use your head, wear safety glasses, and protect your hearing. I have shot the rockets for years and have yet to get hurt; but if you're careless, someone could easily get hurt.

Step 3: Construction—Part 1

Glue both clean out caps on the pipes. Make sure they're pressed on all the way. *Do not* glue the other caps on yet.

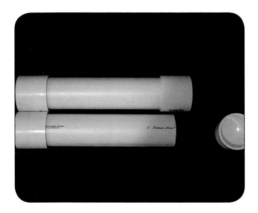

Step 4: Construction—Part 2

Drill a small hole through both of the clean out fittings. Make sure the fittings are lined up and you don't drill where the caps thread in. Bolt the two sides together, finger tight. Later, you will have to loosen it.

Step 5: Construction—Part 3

Place the front caps on the pipe. You may have to shorten the capped bottom pipe by an inch to make it easy enough to remove. Lay the pipes on their sides on a level surface and drill a hole for a nut and bolt. Make sure the hole is as far forward as possible. You have to glue the bolt in the bottom cap. After the framing is done, bolt or screw the bottom cap on. *Do not glue the cap—* you may need to fix it later.

Step 6: Construction—Part 4

Make sure the two pipes are bolted together. With a hole saw, drill a 2" hole in the back of the top pipe. Make sure that you have clearance for the elbow pipe. After the hole is drilled, glue the elbow pipe in.

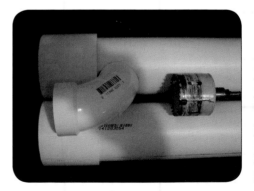

Step 7: Construction—Part 5

Remove the air pump from its housing.

Step 8: Construction—Part 6

Place the air pump in the front of the bottom pipe; you may have to cut a hole for the air pump head in the PVC pipe if it won't fit. The air line should run out the back of the bottom PVC pipe. The power wires should run out the front.

Step 9: Construction—Part 7

If you're using a piezo igniter, you can skip Steps 8 and 9.

Note: Piezo igniters don't work as well as a coil. You will need a coil that will fit in the PVC pipe; a motorcycle coil will work best.

Step 10: Construction—Part 8

Place the coil in front of the air pump. The high voltage lead/spark plug wire should run out the back. The low voltage wires should run out the front.

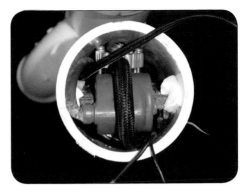

Step 11: Construction—Part 9

Relay and hook up all wiring in front according to chart 1. If you're using a piezo igniter, you don't use a relay. The relay is used to make a continuous spark.

Step 12: Construction—Part 10

Drill three holes about 2" apart for pressure gauge, switch, and primer bulb. If you're using a piezo igniter, drill a another hole for it. Make sure you have room in the pipe where you're drilling.

soda bottle

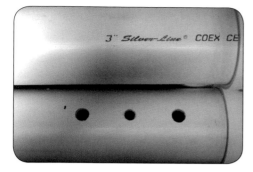

Step 13: Construction—Part 11

Fuel tank: You need to find a fuel tank small enough to fit in the PVC pipe. I used a small ½ oz car vacuum chamber. This oz will gave me about forty to fifty shots.

Step 14: Construction—Part 12

Install your fuel tank wherever you have room. Remember that you have to fit a battery in later. You should have your coil and air compressor wiring coming out the back of the bottom PVC pipe. Depending upon where your fuel tank is mounted, now might be a good time to install it. Make sure you have a way to fill it.

Step 15: Construction—Part 13

Install the gauge, switch, primer bulb, and, if used, piezo igniter. It may be easier to wire up the switch before installing it. The same goes for the gauge and primer bulb.

Step 16: Construction—Part 14

Due to how different the parts you may be using are, you're on your own on this step. The main goal is to run the fuel and the ground line through the air line to the launcher. Make sure you run the ground, fuel, and air line 3'. One end of the tee goes to the gauge, while the other two go to the pump and launcher. Note: Go heavy on the super glue!

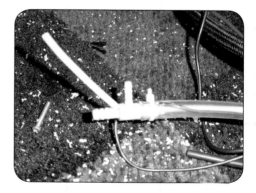

Step 17: Construction—Part 15

Drill two holes in the bottom back clean out: one for the air line, the other for the spark plug wire. The other line is for filling the gas tank.

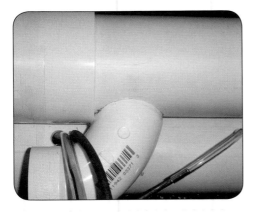

Step 18: Construction— Part 16

Install the wiring according to chart 1. Connect the one-way valve to the fuel line entering the air line. The other end goes to the primer bulb output. The primer bulb input comes from the bottom of the gas tank. All the grounds and negatives are shared. Leave room for the battery.

Step 19: Construction— Part 17

Cut the copper tubing about ½" longer than the ½" plastic pipe, about 12.5". You can solder a barb fitting on the copper pipe for the hose, but keep the length at 12.5". Solder the igniter end closed (refer to chart 2). Put a small

pin hole in the copper tubing right below the solder. The black mark is how far the fuel line comes up in the copper air line.

Step 20: Construction— Part 18

Drill a hole in one of the caps so that the pipe can thread into it. Make sure it is centered, then glue it.

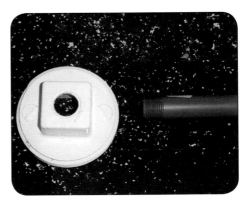

Step 21: Construction— Part 19

You can use less than 3' (2.5'should work) of the tubing and spark plug wire. Just make sure you have enough to unscrew the launcher with a bottle on it. Run the fuel line up through the copper tube about 2.5" from the top. Connect the air line to the bottom of the copper tube. You have to cut some of the air line to do this (refer to chart 2). Cut the ground line the same length as the air line. Splice the wire and connect it to the copper tube. Run the spark plug wire

47

along the copper tube stopping about 1.25" from the top. Glue the spark plug wire to the copper tube. Insert a piece of piano wire in the center of the spark plug wire sticking out about 1.25". Put a small bend at the top towards the copper tube. After all measurements are made, glue the air line to the copper tube with super glue.

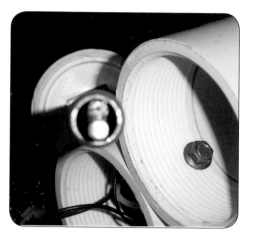

Step 22: Construction—Part 20

Put the copper tube and spark plug wire through the ½" plastic pipe. The copper pipe should stick out about ½". Fill the end with hot glue.

Step 23: Construction—Part 21

Put a bottle in the PVC pipe to hold the ½" pipe straight while the glue dries.

Step 24: Construction—Part 22

Use a hose clamp as a stopper for your bottle so it does not hit the igniter.

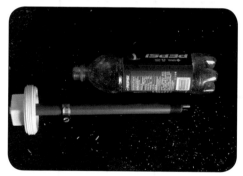

Step 25: Construction—Part 23 (IMPORTANT!)

Wipe super glue around the base of the launcher starting at the pipe clamp going up about 1.5", *let it dry*, then check the fit of the bottle in the glued area. It should fit fairly tight and, when tested with air pressure, it should come off with about 50 PSI. The idea is to keep the bottle in place while being pressurized to 35 PSI. When it is fired, the pressure will well exceed 50 PSI and the bottle will release. *Do not glue the bottle on the pipe!* If the bottle is too tight, it may explode when fired. If the bottle does explode, most of the time, it just blows the front of the bottle off with a loud bang. If it fails to fire, *do not get in front of the barrel*. Wait a few minutes, unscrew the back, and remove the bottle.

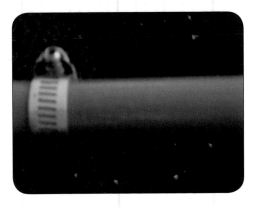

Step 26: Fire!

Make sure there is no bottle on the launcher. Fill the gas tank by turning it upside down, putting the filling hose in gas, and pumping the primer bulb until all the air is out of the line and gas starts to run out of the copper tube. Make sure you don't have a bottle on the launcher. Run the air pump to expel any excess gas from the vaporizer assembly. Now you can put the bottle on the launch tube and press down until it hits the stopper. Pump the primer bulb halfway and you should see the fuel run into the vaporizer tubes. Turn the compressor on and pressurize the bottle to 25–35 PSI. Any higher is at your own risk. Fire!

Again, run the air pump to get rid of excess gas from the vaporizer assembly. Place the bottle on the launch tube and press down until it hits the stopper. Repeat pumping the primer bulb halfway so that the fuel runs into the vaporizer tubes. Turn the compressor on and pressurize the bottle to 25–35 PSI. If it does not fire, don't get in front of the launcher. Wait a few minutes, then unscrew the launch tube and remove and replace the bottle (the bottle may

be flooded). Try putting a few ounces of water in the bottle: this will give you a nice boost. You can also shoot this from the hip if you feel confident enough after a few firings. I don't, however, advise shooting from your shoulder unless you devise some facial shielding or other protection.

Step 27: Tray

The bottles don't carry too far (due to their weight) but they're not supposed to. The object on the front (water balloon, etc.) is the payload. You have to make a launching tray out of another soda bottle. Just chop the bottom off about a fourth of the way up. You can also put water in the rocket bottle (about ¼ full) for some extra kick. Do not fire objects over 6 oz. Wear safety glasses and ear plugs. And, most of all, use your head! Think about where you are and who is around when you decide to start firing!

49

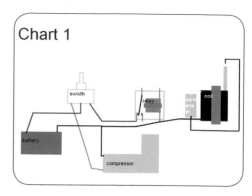

Chart 1

Chart 2

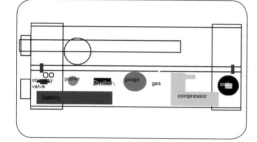

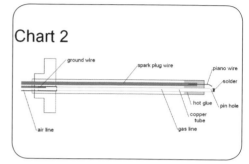

Professional Water Rocket Guide

By: oscarthompson
(http://www.instructables.com/
id/Professional-water-rocket-
guide/)

This Instructable will show you the how to build and fly water rockets, featuring two-stage rockets and drop away boosters along with some basics. This Instructable is based the knowledge of water rockets that I have learned in the past few years.

I am not responsible for any damage you inflict on yourself or others from launching or building water rockets. Have fun building and flying!

Materials
- 3 1.25-liter bottles
- A ping pong ball
- Fin template
- Cardboard
- A plumbing coupling

Tools
- A craft knife
- Plastic adhesive glue (or tape)
- Sealant glue
- Drill

Step 1: Let's Get Started

A water rocket is propelled by pressurized air forcing water down though a nozzle. This creates thrust.

If you took a standard two liter soft drink bottle and pressurized it to 120 PSI, the rocket would reach about 100 or so feet. But then if you took two 2-liter bottles and pressurized them to 120 PSI again, the rocket would go about 150 feet or so, because the rocket has more air in it and creates more thrust. The rocket will only go 50 feet more because of the added mass. You can stop this by making a two stage rocket. A two stage rocket will work better because it would not have to carry the full payload on all of its flight.

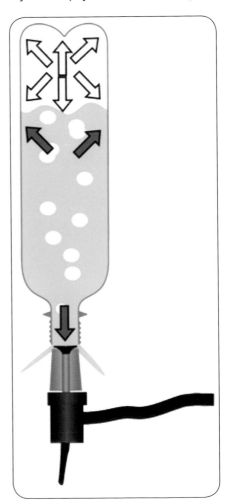

Step 2: How to Build Fins and Nose Cones

In the next few steps, you will be shown how to build the basic needs of a bottle rocket. This step is to get a good understanding of what a rocket needs. Cut the top and bottom off of a 1.25 liter bottle. Then cut the neck off the top.

Step 3: Nose Cone—Part 1

Cut a ping pong ball in half with a craft knife. Glue half of the ping pong ball into the top of the 1.25 liter bottle top. Use a plastic adhesive glue. If appearance doesn't matter, you could just tape it on!

Step 4: Nose Cone–Part 2

Glue or tape the nose cone to the top of the rocket. Adding weight to the nose cone may help. It will move the centre of gravity higher, thus making it more stable.

Step 5: Fins

This stage till involves the basics of how to make a water rocket but may help in later projects. Copy the fin template at the end of the project or design your own. Then, glue the fin template onto cardboard and cut it out or use it as a template for correguted plastic.

Step 6: Attach the Fins

soda bottle

You can attach the fins by
1. Gluing them on
2. Taping them on

To glue correx fins to the rocket use, PL premium or a plastic glue. To glue cardboard fins on, use PL premium or gorilla glue.

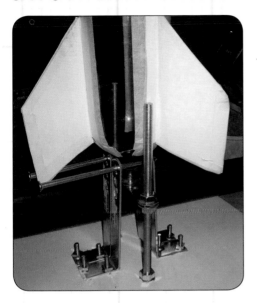

Step 7: Now for the Professional Water Rockets

Professional water rockets can vary from big one-stage rockets to two-stage rockets with drop away boosters. This stage of the Instructable will show you how to make a big one stager and how to couple or splice bottles together.

To couple bottles, first drill a hole about 7–8 mm in width in the bottom of one of your bottles. Next, screw the male end of a plumbing coupling, which is about 8 mm in width, into the bottom of the bottle, then seal it with a sealant glue. Next drill an 8 mm hole in the other bottle cap and then insert the male end into it. Whist the bottle cap is off the bottle, screw the female end into the other side of the bottle cap (side facing the inside). If you want, you can seal it with glue as well.

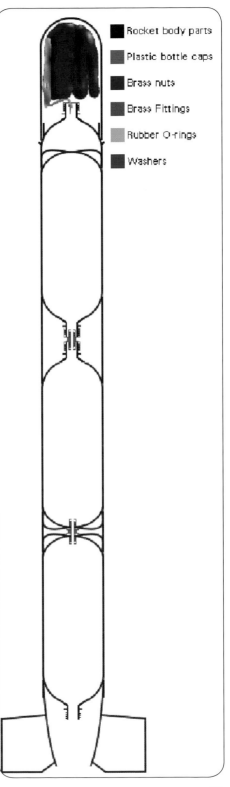

Rocket body parts
Plastic bottle caps
Brass nuts
Brass Fittings
Rubber O-rings
Washers

soda bottle

53

Step 8: Splicing

To join two bottles together like in the picture to create an air tight seal, you need three bottles. First, cut the bottom ends off two of the same sized bottles. Then cut both ends of the same sized third bottle and place that in the two exposed ends of the bottle. Next glue the third bottle in the two exposed ends.

- 1 10mm metal drill bit
- 1 10mm wood drill bit
- 6 10mm nuts and washers
- 1 presta bike valve (you can get this from an old inner tube)
- 1 rubber bung
- 1 bike pump
- 2 tent pegs
- 4 L-shaped brackets
- 2 nails

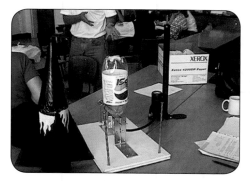

Step 9: Launchers

The laucher that my water rockets are made for was designed by NASA. The launcher lets you vary the nozzle size so you can get better performance from your rocket. The next few steps will show you how to make it.

PDF from NASA below

Step 11: How to Make the Launcher and Nozzles

The launcher can hold any type of pressure depending on the rubber bung. If you have a different nozzle size, then you can adjust the nuts on the bolts so the pins can line up with the hole in the 90° mending plate and the neck of the bottle.

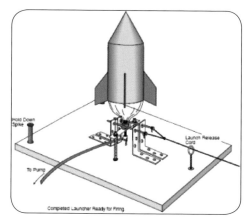

Step 10: Launcher Parts

Below are the materials you will need for the launcher
- 1 ½" wood (any type)
- 2 10mm bolts

Step 12: Two-Stage rockets

The mechanism I use to stage my rocket is different to Air Commands or any other two-stage water rocket. I have tried to make the stager compact. The stager can link to a servo or a pressure switch. The instructions for it are in the next few steps.

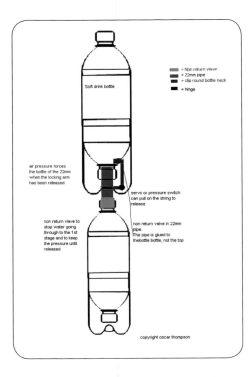

Step 13: Stager
Materials
- 1 22mm pipe, any lenth over 6"
- 1 piece of plywood or plastic (to hold the bottle in place)
- 1 inline, non-return valve (one from a balloon pump will do)
- A first stage of a bottle rocket and a second

Instructions
1. Insert ³⁄₅" of the 6" pipe into the first stage (picture 1).
2. Use epoxy or PVC cement to seal it (picture 1).
3. Insert a non-return valve into the pipe and glue it.
4. Work out the dimensions of how long and wide the plywood or plastic needs to be to hold the bottle in place. Thenc cut it out using picture

2 to help you. The hinge is mounted on the pipe clamp.
5. When you slide the bottle on (use vaseline to seal it), make sure the pipe clamp is right next to the neck on the first stage. This will have your hinge on. Next, clip your hinge onto the bottle neck so it is tight and won't fall off.

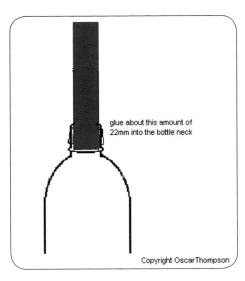

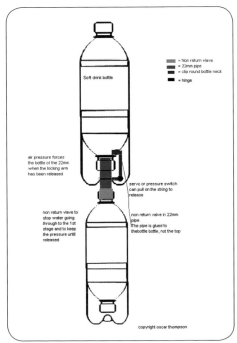

soda bottle

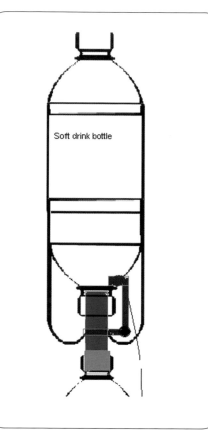

Soft drink bottle

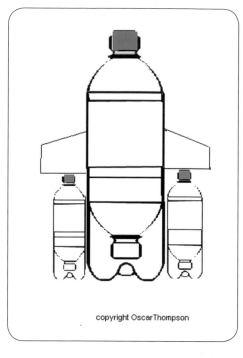

copyright OscarThompson

Step 14: Drop-Away Boosters!

These boosters are easy to make because they are only held on by the upward thrust of the bottles. These drop-away boosters are different to Air Commands. For the drop away boosters, you will have to make three of the launchers. Instructions:

1. Measure your drop-away booster bottles against your main rocket. Make a mark (dot or line) where the top of the booster meets on your rocket.
2. Use picture 1 to help you. Where you marked a dot on the booster, glue the advanced fins together and stick the bottom of the fins on the marked dot with duck tape or glue. The advanced fin template is on step 15.
3. Test the rocket!

Step 15: Advanced Fins

These advanced fins are for bigger rockets and are very good for two-stage rockets and rockets with drop-away boosters. For fins, print off the template below.

56

Step 16: Payloads and Parachutes

The next few steps will show you how to make a parachute system followed on by a payload bay. The parachute system used by me is a simple gravitational deployment. The nose cone is fitted on the rocket loosely and, when the rocket reaches its maximum altitude, the rocket will fall back to earth nose first. Because the nose has a weight in it, it falls off, deploying the parachute inside.

Step 17: Steps for the Parachutes

Find a payload bay for your rocket, any size to fit a parachute. Build a nose cone as shown in steps 2 and 3. Your

nose cone either needs to fit loosely on top of the payload bay or loosely in it. Cut a hole in the payload bay and the nose cone so a string can fit though it and be knotted. Tie the parachute string to the string you have tied to the nose cone and the payload bay.

soda bottle

Step 18: Steps for the Payload

Payloads are used to carry equipment such as altitude meters, accelerometers, or even a slug. Cut the bottom off any size bottle. Cut two disks the same width as the bottle out of corrugated plastic. Now, cut a strip out of plastic the same width as the bottle but a little bit smaller in length than the bottle. Glue them together and, when dry, put your payload into the payload section of the rocket.

soda bottle

Step 19: Rocket designs

You are free to look at these pictures if you need help for a design.

booster
air

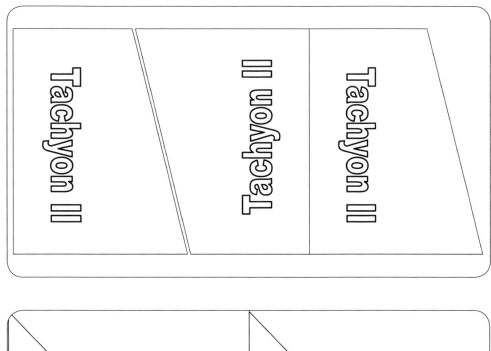

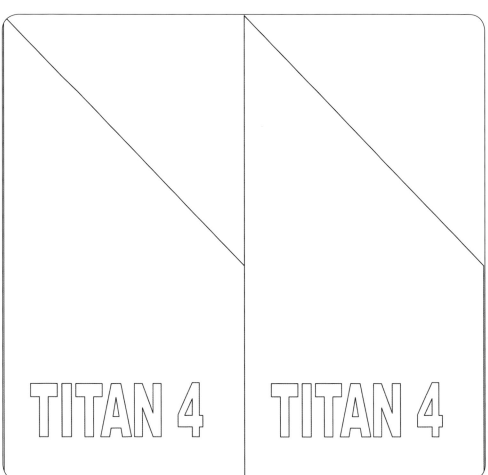

soda bottle

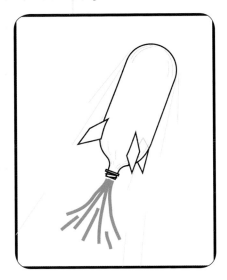

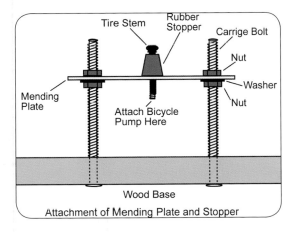

Tire Stem
Rubber Stopper
Carrige Bolt
Nut
Washer
Nut
Mending Plate
Attach Bicycle Pump Here
Wood Base

Attachment of Mending Plate and Stopper

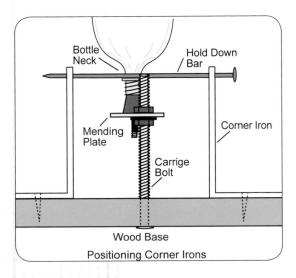

Bottle Neck
Hold Down Bar
Mending Plate
Corner Iron
Carrige Bolt
Wood Base

Positioning Corner Irons

soda bottle

61

soda bottle

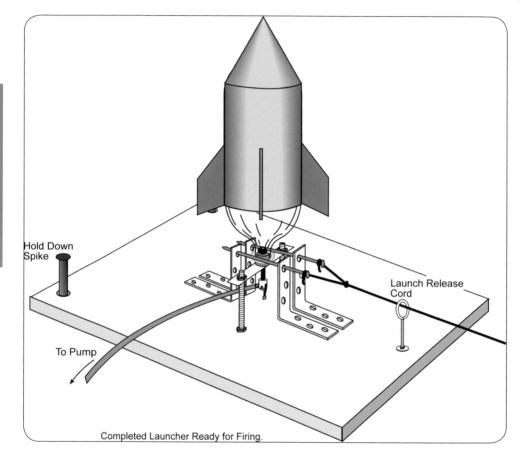

Hold Down
Spike

Launch Release
Cord

To Pump

Completed Launcher Ready for Firing.

Rocket Eggstronaut Project

By: stumitch
(http://www.instructables.com/id/A-Rocket-Eggstronaut-Project/)

I've seen all sorts of water bottle rockets on Instructables and while surfing the web, but I thought an Instructable with the step-by-step process of building a whole bunch of them with a class of grade six kids would be good. Each step in the Instructable will be a day in the class. At the top of each day, you'll find a list of tools and materials. Just follow through a day in advance and you'll have kids learning so much more than anyone bargained for.

This rocket is based on the usual 2-liter pop bottle you find at grocery stores. You add water and pressurized air and, using these instructions, you'll get height that you and your students will not believe. To make it interesting, we have a passenger . . . the Eggstronaut. This is an egg that, if it survives, will award extra marks to the team.

You'll need the basic materials listed below as well as a launcher. A good hand pump works, well but a compressor *really* makes life easy. You can maximize the pressure like crazy, too.

Learning Objectives:
- The students will learn and apply Newton's Second Law of Motion in a way that makes sense to them.
- "The more massive an object is . . . the more force it takes to accelerate it." Or you could say, "Heavy stuff takes more force to move."

- The students will learn and apply the basic principles of Newton's Third Law of Motion. "To every action there is an equal and opposite reaction." Or you could say, "If you push something, it will push back."
- The students will understand Newton's First Law of Motion: "F=MA." Or, to make it so I can understand, "Stuff that is sitting there will stay that way unless something happens to it. Once things start moving, they tend to keep moving until something happens to change how it is moving."
- Students will learn to tell the difference between *mass* and *size*.
- By building a simple rocket, the students will understand these laws in a way that makes sense to them. They will also learn to think creatively, design, and

problem solve while building a basic design.

- The students will learn to use basic tools to construct a working project.

Tools and Materials:

- Scissors
- Hot glue gun
- Duct tape
- X-acto or Olfa mat knife
- 2-liter pop bottles (*not* water bottles!). Get at least two of them.
- Cardboard or coroplast (the stuff cheap signs are made of)
- Batting, foam, paper strips (whatever you find for the Eggstronaut)
- egg

Vocabulary:

- **Pressurizing**
- **Ratio**
- **Symmetrical**
- **Hypotenuse**
- **Scale** (as in drawing to scale)

I'll also provide a marking sheet at the end so you can use it in your class.

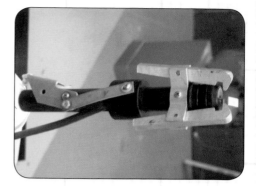

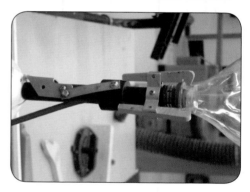

Step 1: Day 1—The Introduction

Tools and Materials:

- A couple of 2-liter bottles
- Big sheets of paper (I cut stuff off a roll from the art guys.)
- Metersticks or yardsticks
- Lots of pencils
- An egg
- A computer with examples of water-bottle rockets from the web (check out YouTube)

After you show the kids examples from the web they will be hard to hold back. It's pretty cool. I start asking questions like these:

- How does it fly?
- Why are some short and some long?
- Some rockets have two fins, some have six. Why?
- What about the fin size?

I cover each of these points on the board. What you want to coax out of them is: The rockets fly by pressurizing air with water. This is important because the "booster bottle," which is pressurized, *must* be a bottle for carbonated drinks and *must not* be punctured or cut at all. It will explode if otherwise. I've done it and it is really scary. Funny, but scary.

Long rockets (double length) work best. You can chat about what **ratio** is now. Suggest methods of lengthening the rocket (tubes, extra bottles, etc.).

Two to four fins that are **symmetrical** work best. Keep them small and explain that, because the rockets explode off at more than 100kph, large fins will rip off. A good size is a triangle with **hypotenuse** of 3–7" and bottom edge of 1–3".

Now introduce the Eggstronaut. Explain that, if the passenger survives, they will get extra marks. They love this. Go over padding and protection if you want, but I find the kids come up with the most amazing ideas . . . better than mine! My only stipulation is that they have to make an escape hatch that can be used to insert and remove the Eggstronaut on the field.

Once the kids are ready, I break them into groups of two or three. Don't do four . . . you always get at least one kid who is left in the cold. I pull out the paper and teach them about drawing objects to scale on the paper. You can trace out a bottle or two to help them visualize it.

Spend the remaining time working on design. You'll get a couple groups that finish the drawing in minutes. Just send them back with revisions, measurements, notes, or whatever you can make up. Make sure they draw the fins to size and that they are being realistic about the egg and how it will get into the hatch.

Spend some time discussing materials. I ask the kids to bring bottles, long cardboard tubes, cardboard, coroplast, and any packing material they will need. It's up to you. I supply basic tools and tape to build the rocket with.

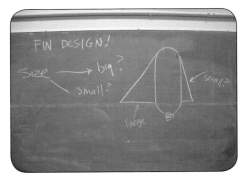

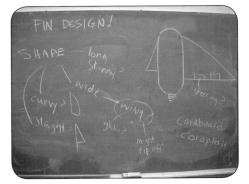

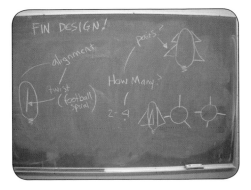

soda bottle

Step 2: Day 2—Building and Newton's Second and Third Laws

Tools and Materials:

- Duct tape
- Hot glue and hot gue guns (optional)
- 2-liter bottles
- Cardboard and coroplast
- Scissors, X-acto knife, mat knives, etc.
- Material for batting
- 2 skateboards (if you can find them)

The kids are ready to build, but first you can do a fun demo. The first law I teach about is Newton's 2nd Law: "The more massive an object is . . . the more force it takes to accelerate it." In other words, "Heavy stuff takes more force to move."

I like to demonstrate this by pulling up the smallest kid in the class. I pull out two skateboards, facing each other and about 2' apart. I put the student on one skateboard and I stand on the other. I'm not a big guy, but usually the size discrepancy is pretty obvious. I longboard as a hobby, but I act like I've never stood on one. I ask the student to hold out both hands in front, and I do the same. I ask the class what would happen if we pushed our hands together really hard. Of course, the kids know what happens, so I gently push on the hands of the student. It's amazing how far a kid will roll. I won't move more than a couple of inches.

I get the kids to notice two things.
- The person with less mass moved further
- The person with more mass still moved a little bit.

Newton's 2nd law relates to the idea that objects with more mass will take more energy to accelerate or move. The person with less mass moved more because it takes less energy to move them. The other part of the demo is that the person with more mas still moved.

This is explained by Newtons 3rd law which says: "To every action, there is an equal and opposite reaction." In other words, "if you push something, it will push back."

The kids notice that I move as well. You could explain the idea that, every time objects move each other, *both* have the same force being pushed on them. Objects with more mass don't *move* as much, but they still have the same energy exerted on them. This is also a good explanation for why we add water to the bottle. The water being pushed out from the bottle has more mass than air, so it pushes against the bottle harder, which forces the bottle up with more force. You can tie this into Newton's 2nd law as well if the kids are still engaged at this point.

Now you can start building stuff! Pull out the drawings, gather the materials, and demonstrate a couple of skills.

Stacking Bottles for Height

Show how to cut a bottle safely with a blade. Keep the cap on when starting (makes it easier). I cut a bottle open about 4" up from the bottom and then show how they can stack. It's up to you if you want the kids to use blades. It worries me, so I ask the kids to use scissors *after* I start the cut for them.

Taping

I give out a yard at a time. Kids will use a whole roll if left to it. I demonstrate how much tougher and more accurate it is to use 4" strips of tape placed lengthwise. I do one side, line up for symmetry, and then tape the other.

Using Drawings as Patterns

I ask the kids to use the drawings as a pattern to cut out the fins and other parts. I find a scroll saw works great on cardboard and coroplast.

Attaching Stuff to the Bottles

Use sandpaper to scuff up wherever they want to attach things. Hot glue works well, but I find that it is used *way* too much and kids tend to burn themselves. Tape works well. The fins can also be taped on with care.

Remind the kids about a couple of things. They forget that the egg has to go in and out easily. I cut a hatch in the top bottle. Remind the students that they *must not* puncture the booster bottle at all. Usually one

team will forget this. You will also get at least one team that will forget that the booster bottle goes *top down* and they will tape the fins on upside down. Make sure they understand **symmetry** and that the rockets work really well if they are about two times the length of a bottle.

soda bottle

So how does this relate to the rockets? I explain that a slightly heavier rocket will go further. A *way* heavier rocket will not move at all, of course. I suggest that weight in the nose can be beneficial, but can be used *only* if it is not sharp, too heavy, or potentially dangerous. A Ziploc of sand works really well. You can tell the kids this, but they come up with great stuff on their own. One team used peanut butter, which is heavy and also worked well as a protector for the egg.

I've included a series of shots that I use to demonstrate the process to the kids. The steps show how you can add two bottles together with just a bit of duct tape. You can also use the duct tape to attach some fins. Notice also that I added water to the top (non-booster bottle).

Step 3: Day 3—Building and Newton's First Law

Tools and materials are the same as Day 2. Today, I like to start with another bit of theory. I verbally test the class to make sure they remember Newton's Second and Third Laws. Then, I introduce the First Law: "F=MA." In other words, "Stuff that is sitting there will stay that way unless something happens to it. Once things start moving, they tend to keep moving until something happens to change how it is moving."

I ask, "What would happen to the student with less mass if *nothing* was slowing them down. The students usually know that the kid would keep moving. We talk a bit about why the student stops (friction, mainly).

Now I ask them, if both the small kid and I started moving at the same speed, who would go farther? They know intuitively that I would, but why? This is where the "M" in the First Law comes in. Explain that force ("F") would increase if the mass ("M") increased. Show them simple examples on the board.

I have kids work out plans for parachutes sometimes. They are pretty exciting for kids and sometimes work, but they need to be carefully planned. Most kids get a plastic bag, tape it to the nose, and hope it will work. It won't. If you want to explore the idea of parachutes, I suggest using plastic bags cut open and tethered properly. I've had students use a bottle cut in half, with the egg attached to the top. The bottle rests on the booster rocket but is not attached. When the rocket is accelerating, the egg bottle remains in place. When the rocket starts to slow, the air pushes the bottle off and the parachute opens.

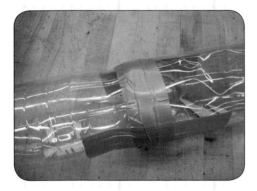

Step 4: Day 4—THE LAUNCH

I make sure the students understand the idea of adding water, as it relates to the laws of motion. It seems that the ideal amount of water is about a third of the bottle, but encourage the kids to experiment.

I bring out the Eggstronauts with much fanfare and excitement. It's fun to turn it into a goofy event. The teams submit the rocket and Eggstronaut hatch for entry. Once the water is added and the egg is in place, we launch. Make sure the kids are well back. Sometimes the rockets go sideways. The most concern for safety comes when a team builds a really accurate rocket. This means the rocket is going to come down pretty much where everyone is standing. If this happens, I get the kids to all make sure they have a back to the wall of the school. This really cuts down on the danger level. Do not let kids run after the rocket until it lands. They have a really solid punch; sometimes they leave holes in the ground.

The biggest concern for me has turned out to be the least. I was worried at first about the bottles exploding. After accidentally exploding a water bottle and a compromised pop bottle on two occasions, I can tell you the only danger is the embarrassment of needing to clean your shorts afterward. It explodes with a very impressive gunshot that scared the heck out of me both times. My guess is that, because the material is so light, it has very little momentum and doesn't cause damage other than evaporating whatever is attached to the bottle. It's pretty impressive!

I give a basic mark related to the design. It needs to look like the rocket when finished. I also give marks for accurate flight and height and a bonus mark for Eggstronaut survival.

Try this project! I've done it for years and I have twenty-year-old ex-students come back and tell me they learned more with the rockets than half their

science classes. As a shop teacher, there really is no greater compliment.

soda bottle

Smart Rocket
By: Spyder2021
(http://www.instructables
.com/id/SMART-ROCKET-By-
Spyder2021/)

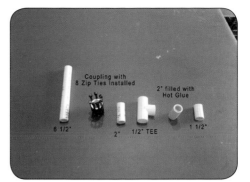

I am going to show you how to build a smart rocket bottle launcher. Everything was built using PVC40 PE PIPE and attachments. You can purchase the supplies from any hardware store; I got mine from Home Depot. The reason why I call it a "smart rocket" is because it uses the Smart Water bottle (and it is longer than a normal pop bottle).

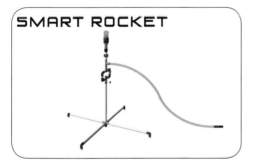

Step 1: Assemble the Top

Never glue the PVC pipe together until you have the entire unit built. As far as the zip ties go: You want to fit the bottle you are using down the 6.5" pipe up to the coupling. Place the zip tie on the rim of the bottle to see what the length of the zip tie you would need is. Assemble them in this order:

- 6.5" section of pipe
- ½" coupling (with zip ties taped to the coupling)
- 2" section of pipe
- ½" Tee
- 2" section of pipe (filled with hot glue)
- 1.5" section of pipe (goes on middle part of Tee)

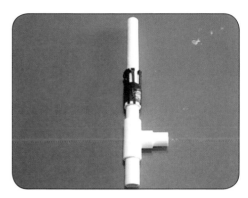

Step 2: Assemble the Middle

You will need to drill a small $^{13}/_{64}$" hole into each ½" Tee as shown. Plus, you will need to get a $^7/_8$" wood spade bit for the top Tee. Drill it all the way through from left to right. For the bottom Tee, drill it from the bottom connection hole right through the top. What this will do is allow you to be able to spin it freely. When done, insert each binding ost through their holes (making sure the binding post is sticking out).

On the Top Tee.

1. Drill a $^7/_8$" hole right through the Tee from left to right (so the PVC and Tee spin easily).
2. Drill a $^{13}/_{64}$" hole in the middle of the Tee and install the binding post, making sure the post sticks through the hole. Then screw in the eye bolt.
3. On the 4.25" PVC pipe, taper one end of the pipe so it is easier to slide through. With the binding

71

post being in the way, it will make it somewhat of a challenge.

4. Do the same for the bottom Tee, except put the ⅞" hole through the middle of the Tee all the way through the backside, making it so the PVC pipe can slide right through.

5. Then assemble the rest as shown.

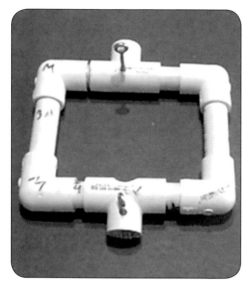

Step 3: Assemble the Bottom

1. Take your ½" PVC cross, and drill a ⅞" hole right through the center.
2. Now you have two pipes at 2' long each; these are for the legs.
3. Take the legs and attach one elbow to either end. Now attach a 1.5" pipe to the other end of the elbow.
4. Place your coupling at the bottom of your 2.5' PVC pipe (we will be using that for the middle shaft). It will go right below the PVC cross.

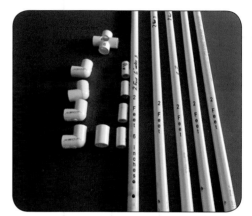

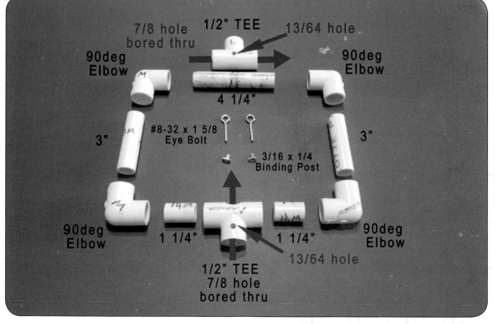

soda bottle

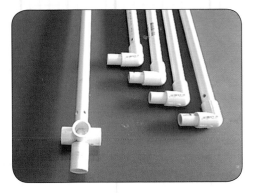

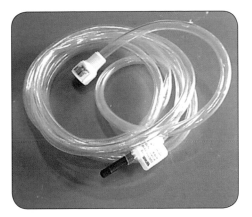

Step 4: Assemble the Hose

This part is really easy. You will need an air valve stem (I purchased one that was 2" long, which allowed more room to fit into the tubing).

1. If needed, cut off the back end of the valve stem, and slide it into one end of the tubing.
2. For the other end of the tubing, slide it through the small hole on the ½" male adapter (push it through a bit, about flush with the male adapter's larger hole). You will want to back fill the adapter around the tubing. Make sure you don't get any glue *in* the tubing. Also, make sure the tubing doesn't close up on you, as the hot glue will soften the tubing until it's cooled.

Step 5: Final Assembly

Here, we will now put together the top, middle, bottom, and tubing.

1. Place the top part into the top of the middle section in the Tee.
2. Slide one of the little rings (cut from a ½" coupling) on the middle shaft. Then, slide the middle shaft through the bottom Tee. (The binding post *will* be in the way; it is best to taper the top of the shaft.) This will still require some force to get it through.
3. Once through, slide another ring (cut from a ½" coupling) on top of the Tee (so it will not move).

soda bottle

Monkey Grip
Tire Valve
2" Long

1 1/2" Male
Adapter

10 feet WATTS Vinyl Tubing
1/2" x 3/8" x 10'

4. Now, attach all four legs to the cross. (The part of the legs that have the 90° elbows and the small pipe attached will not go into the cross). The bare part of the 2' PVC pipe goes into each hole of the cross.

5. Attach the male adapter to the *top* part of the launcher (fitting over the PVC pipe that is sticking out).

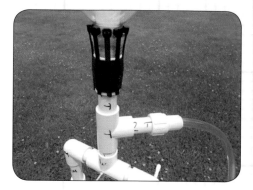

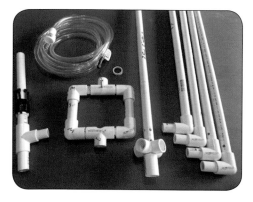

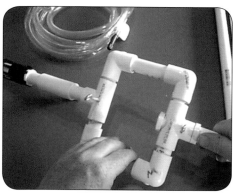

Step 6: Re-Cap with Pictures

Okay, now that you have the entire thing built, you can start gluing the parts that don't move.Or you can just leave them the way they are. Here are some pictures of the final product.

Just slide your Smart Bottle down the 6.5" pipe and it will lock into the zip ties. Apply air either with a bike pump or an air compressor via the valve stem and watch it fly.

Added up, this project cost me $25 tops.

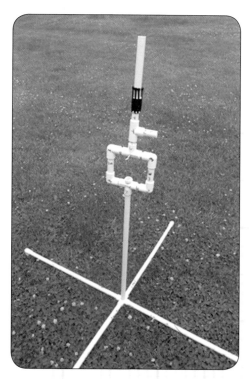

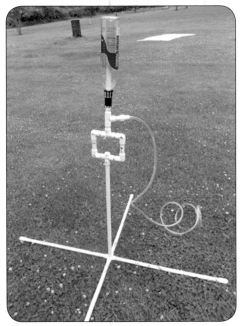

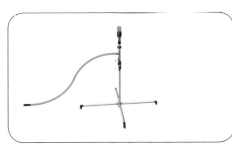

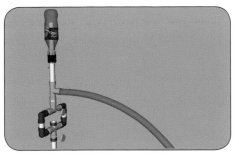

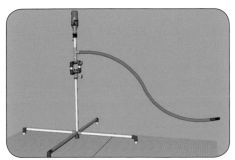

soda bottle

75

Soda Bottle Water Rocket

By: cyenobite
(http://www.instructables.com/
id/Soda-Bottle-Water-Rocket/)

In a couple of hours (or less), you could make this water rocket! Water rockets use water and pressurized air to launch a soda bottle hundreds of feet into the air. This Instructable will *not* cover the launcher. There are many websites with water rocket plans (and launchers); part of the fun is to experiment and come up with your own designs. Feel free to modify, improve, and experiment with thisIinstructable. The original inspiration for this rocket was from the magazine called MAKE Magazine (makezine.com).

Step 1: Materials
- 2 soda bottles (empty) (Note: There are slight differences in the openings of the bottle depending on the soda brand. Pepsi is just a tad smaller than Coke. This Instructable is set up for 2-liter sized bottles—feel free to adjust for any size though.)
- 1 sharp knife (Kids, get your parents help here!) I prefer X-acto brand for cutting foam core.
- 1 large sheet of foam core (I prefer black, but any color will do). Foam core can be found at almost any arts and crafts supply store. To learn more about foam core, try Wikipedia.

- 5-minute epoxy (This stuff is nasty! Do not inhale, and use in a well ventilated area. Do *not* get it on your skin, eyes, or hair, etc. Read all safety warnings before using.) Feel free to experiment with other glues. This can usually be found at any hardware store—kids, ask your parents for help with this glue.
- 2 (or more) markers—I used Sharpies, one black and one silver.
- Clear shipping tape It's thicker than regular scotch tape and about 2" wide.)
- 2 (or more) cans of spray paint—pick your own favorite colors!

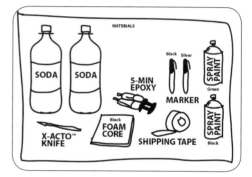

Step 2: Cut Bottle
Peel all labels off of the bottles. Measure up from the bottle about a Third and cut the bottle. Try to keep your cut line as straight as possible. It may help to mark a straight line around the bottle first. Be sure to recycle or reuse any scrap pieces.

soda bottle

Step 3: Bottle Merge

Take the cut bottle from the previous step and insert it directly over the bottom of the other bottle—this becomes the nose cone of the rocket. Try your best to keep everything straight. If you put the nose on crooked, your rocket will fly crooked. Place the nose cone on loosely at first, then gently press down until firm. Turn the bottle upside down and let it drop on a hard surface several times. If you press the nose cone on too hard, you'll start to get "crinkles" in the plastic. Crinkles are bad.

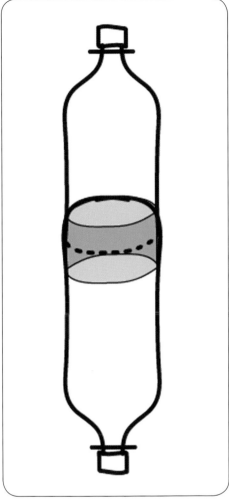

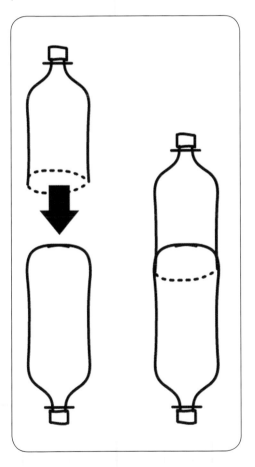

Step 4: Tape Bottles Together

Once the nose cone is on tight (but not too tight), use the clear shipping tape to tape the seams. Try to keep the tape smooth.

Step 5: Cut the Fins

Next you have to cut some fins to keep your rocket flying straight. At the end of this Instructable are fins I designed, so you can use those as a template. I used a Pepsi bottle, so again, you may need to adjust the curves to fit your bottle. Kids, this is the step that you will need your parents' help. Parents, cutting foam core can be tricky. The key is to cut one time all the way through in a smooth motion. You'll need to press hard to make sure the knife is all the way through the foam core. If you feel more comfortable using a utility knife, by all means do so. Be careful! Please!

soda bottle

Experiment with your own fin designs. I chose a more squared off design, but you can use curves if you like. You'll need a minimum of three fins, but no more than four (unless you really, really want to!). If you do three, you need to split your bottle into thirds, which equals 120°. Also at the end of this Instructable is a 120 degree template. For four fins, you'll just need 90°.

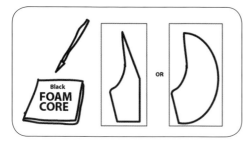

Step 6: Fin Supports

This step may not be needed, but I figured better safe than sorry. Using some of the scrap pieces of foam core, I cut six small triangles (approximately 1" × 1.5"). These will be added to your fins later for extra support.

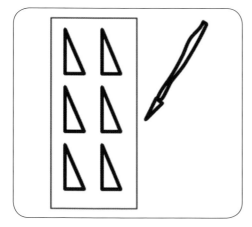

Step 7: Attaching the Fins

Okay, this is the tricky part. Open your adhesive (or glue of your choice). Squeeze out a small amount (enough to do one fin). Mix the epoxy with a scrap piece of foam core (this will be your "brush," too). Pre-mark your bottle (with the marker) where you want your fins to line up. Make sure the fins fit your bottle *before* putting any glue on them. Trim or adjust if needed. Apply the epoxy to your fin, and attach it to the bottle.

WARNING: This step requires patience! Five minutes is a *long* time. If you can figure out a way of setting up some clamps, more power to you. While holding the fin, don't let it shift. You will be able to move and adjust the fin while the epoxy is drying, but, once it starts to set, it gets difficult to adjust. You'll feel it start to set. Once it gets to the point where you can't really adjust it anymore, you can place the bottles and fin on the table to set without holding it. Prepare your next "glob" of glue for the next fin. Repeat for all of your fins.

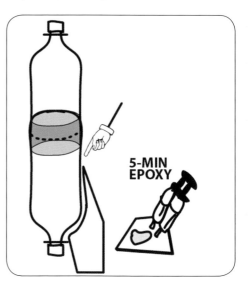

5-MIN EPOXY

Step 8: Glue Your Fin Supports

This is the added step for extra support. Glob out another dab of epoxy and glue your triangle to the bottle and the fin. Glue the supports on each side of each fin. Wait approximately 10—15 minutes to be sure the epoxy has set. Guess what. You're done with all of the assembly at this point! You could take this rocket to the launcher at this stage and let it rip! But it's kind of messy looking isn't it? One more step . . .

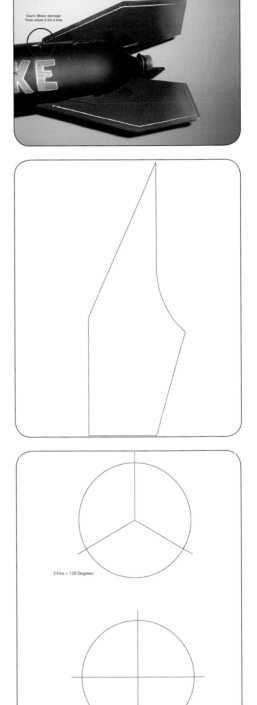

Step 9: Paint and Details

This is where the spray paint comes in. I used black and a bright green, so that the rocket would be easy to spot while up in the air! Decorate your rocket any way you like! Flames, spots, checkers, glitter, etc. Use your extra markers to add any fine details or words (I put H20 on mine so everyone would know this is a water rocket).

Note: as you can see from this photo, I also added some additional tape to the fins for extra support. Do this *before* painting. Perhaps, I should have mentioned this before, but this rocket has no parachute! What goes up must come down. WARNING: *Do not* launch this rocket near people, a crowd, small animals, streets, cars, or houses. In other words, take your rocket out to the middle of nowhere and launch it in a safe place. Make sure everyone knows there is no parachute and that this rocket will be crashing to earth at a high rate of speed. I wouldn't want to get hit by it! The rocket will probably fly higher and farther than you think.

soda bottle

Section 4

Chemically Powered Rockets

Black Powder Rockets and DIY Tooling

By: NightHawkInLight
(http://www.instructables.com/
id/How-to-Make-Black-Powder-
Rockets-DIY-Tooling/)

After I got into pyrotechnics, I avoided rocketry for quite a while. It was not that I found rockets less enjoyable to watch than other forms of pyrotechnics; I simply believed they required a large array of expensive tools and, therefore, passed them over because I was more interested in spending that money on chemicals for building big and impressive shells.

It took years of envying others who could build rockets, and watching the soft lift into the sky, before I realized that I preferred shells lifted in that manner to those that are blasted out of a mortar. That realization forced me to reconsider rocketry as something I would like to experiment with.

I was still unwilling to spend hundreds of dollars on commercially made tooling for something I wasn't even sure if I would enjoy, so my only option was to make tooling myself. Black powder rockets are the safest type of rocket to make and use, and the simplest to perfect, so they proved to be the best type to start with.

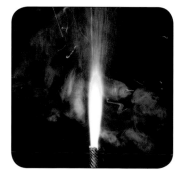

Step 1: Making the Tooling

This tooling is made for rockets with an engine 4.5" in length and ¾" in internal diameter. With the aid of a bench grinder, a drill, and a few grades of sandpaper, it turned out to be quite easy to shape a spindle out of a ⅜" × 4.5" threaded brass rod. With masking tape protecting the threads, the rod is chucked into the drill and spun at high speeds while in contact with the grinding wheel. This keeps the amount of material ground off the rod spread evenly around the circumference. A slight taper is given to the rod, with the thickest part toward the threads that are chucked in the drill, and tapered down to about half the starting diameter at the tip. The thickest part at the bottom should be just narrow enough that all evidence of the threads is sanded down. To make the tooling correctly, the top 3" of the 4.5" rod are shaped, and the remaining 1.5" is left threaded for the extractor nuts to thread onto.

The bench grinder provides a very course grind, leaving deep scratches in the spindle. Because of that, the spindle needs to be ground down slightly more after the wheel has done the bulk of the shaping (removing the threads, giving the taper). One-hundred-grit sandpaper held against the spindle while the drill spins it does a good job of removing the deep scratches, and 600 grit will give a good polish to the metal. The smooth surface will reduce friction when removing it from a rammed rocket, and leave a solid and undisturbed powder core.

The spindle can now be finished off by placing two nuts onto the threads and tapping the threads on the bottom of the spindle gently to pinch them closed so the bottom nut cannot spin off. A washer is then dropped over the spindle to sit above the two nuts.

The base for the spindle is then formed with three squares of hardwood (oak) measuring 2.5" × 2.5" × ¾".

Two of the blocks are held together and a ⅜" hole is drilled straight through both of them. The top block is then removed and the hole in the lower block is widened to ¾". All three blocks are now stacked on top of each other and clamped to prevent them from shifting— the block with the ⅜" hole on top, the one with a ¾" hole in the middle, and the solid block on the bottom. Now, on opposite corners of the stack, a ⅛" hole is drilled straight through to the bottom block. Through these two new holes, a 3" decking screw is driven in to the point that the threads are dug into the bottom two blocks, but the smooth portion of the screw towards the head is all that remains in the top block. There should be plenty of room that this can occur without sinking the head of the screw into the top block. The heads of the screws are then cut off with a hack saw so that the top block can be removed, leaving the bottom two blocks held together with the smooth shank of the screws sticking out of the two opposite corners. If the points of the screws are sticking out of the underside of the two blocks, those points can now be removed so the tooling sits flat.

The top block of the tooling should now be able to be lined up with the two pins and snapped down onto the tooling, aligned exactly the same way every time.

A small recess 1.25" in diameter should now be drilled around the ⅜" hole on the underside of the top block, so that the washer on the spindle will be able to fit between the top and middle block when the spindle is inserted. That will complete the tooling base.

The threaded end of the spindle, with the two nuts threaded onto it and the washer sitting on top, is now inserted into the ¾" hole in the middle block of the base. The tip of the spindle is threaded through the ⅜" hole in the top block, which is snapped in place.

To form the rammers, ¾" diameter dowels are used. A drill press makes it a simple task to drill out the holes through the longest two rammers for the spindle to feed into. The following lengths of dowel should be used for the three rammers: 5", 3.5", and 2".

The longest rammer needs the full 3" length of the spindle drilled out and the end tapered to form the nozzle. The 3.5" rammer only needs a 2" core, and the shortest should have no core. Even though the threaded rod that the spindle was made of started as ⅜" diameter, after grinding it, it loses quite a bit of that material. Therefore the holes through the rammers can be made smaller than ⅜" diameter, though how much smaller depends on how much of a grind and taper was given by the maker of the tooling.

Step 2: Black Powder Rocket Fuel

The term black powder can be used to describe any pyrotechnic composition composed of the potassium nitrate, charcoal, and sulfur. These three chemicals can be combined in a variety of ratios to fit specific purposes. The traditional mixture that would be used in black powder firearms and pyrotechnic purposes other than rocketry is a ratio of 75 percent potassium nitrate, 15 percent charcoal, 10 percent sulfur, all measured by weight and milled with lead media to make an intimately combined mixture.

This ratio typically burns far too quickly to be used as fuel in cored rockets, a more ideal ratio being 60 percent potassium nitrate, 30 percent charcoal, 10 percent sulfur. If all chemicals are finely powdered, they need not be ball milled, and may simply be mixed together by screening. It is likely that this fuel will work fine in the rockets we are making here. Should it burn too rapidly and cause the rockets to explode, additional charcoal may be added to slow the fuel. If the rockets do not take to the sky but instead burn out on the ground, it is possible that the fuel is burning too slowly, in which case the charcoal in the composition may

be reduced. Increasing and reducing components in a composition can be a tricky process to get right if done too quickly, so when making changes do not add or remove more than 2% of a chemical at a time. This will allow you to dial in the ideal fuel. Be sure to take consistent and thorough notes so any changes that may cause a success or failure are recorded.

Candy Bar (Milky Way®) Rocket Engine

By: killbox

(http://www.instructables.com/
id/Candybar-Milkyway-Rocket-
Engine/)

Quelab (My local Hackerspace in Albuquerque, NM), had a project theme of "Hacking Chocolate" for the month of February. I'm allergic to eating chocolate, so I wanted to think of a use that was a bit more exciting than just watching others eat the stuff.

So I decided to experiment with making a chocolate (candy bar) powered rocket engine. A quick Googling showed me that I was remembering correctly that people make sugar and potassium nitrate rockets (and even Pixy Stix® rockets) I decided to see if I could do it, too, only using a candy bar! (You know how many calories there are in them, right?)

Sticking with a space theme, and avoiding complex compounds such as peanuts, a Milky Way candy bar was just the ticket.

Step 1: Materials and Tools
Materials
- Some clay kitty litter (a few ounces of clean, clay-based kitty litter will do). This will make the fireproof plugs at both ends of the engine.
- A Milky Way candy bar for fuel
- Some potassium nitrate (salt peter; as pure as you can get) oxidizer
- Some thin-wall PVC pipe (about the same internal diameter as the carriage bolt head), cut into 2.5" lengths
- Some cannon fuse or model rocket engine igniter

Tools
- A small scale
- A hammer
- A grinder (mortar and pestle like I show here or a coffee grinder you don't plan to use for food again)
- An anvil, chunk of steel, or other hard object to pound on
- A domed head carriage bolt (I believe the head size of mine was ¾" and it was about 4" long.)
- A drill, with 7 mm drill bit, and a counter sink drill bit (or a larger ½" bit will do too)
- A permanent marker

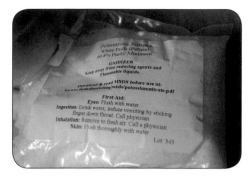

Step 2: Getting Started

Cut the candy bar into 10 g chunks, and toss those chunks into the freezer for a few hours. (This makes it brittle enough to grind well.) While that is freezing, we can start our engine plug and potassium nitrate grind.

Let's start with the engine plug. Measure out about 2 tablespoons of kitty litter into your grinder, and grind into a fine powder. (Due to varying hardness and clumping, there may be bigger chunks in the powder. This is ok—just try to get it at least 60 percent fine powder.)

Note: If these clay/dust cat litter plugs are blowing out, use a pipe de-burring brush inside the pipe. It may scratch the PVC up enough to give the litter a little more to grab onto.

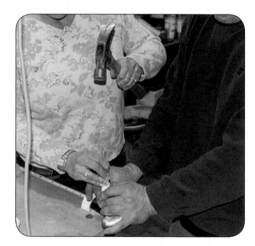

Now take your 2.5" long PVC tube, place it standing up on the anvil, and pour 1 teaspoon of ground kitty litter into it. Slide the round, topped carriage bolthead into the PVC pipe and compact the kitty litter using the hammer. (Give it about ten good whacks so it really compacts together into a solid plug; see second photo.)

Hold the PVC tube up to the light to see how thick it is. You want a plug of ⅗" thick (remember the sides will be higher due to the bolt's head shape). If its thinner, add some more kitty litter and compact using the hammer again. Mark the depth of the plug on the tube using the marker. This will be handy later for drilling/flaring the nozzle.

chemical

Step 3: Grinding

With the candy bar still in the freezer chilling, measure out 25 g of potassium nitrate into the grinder. Grind it into a powdered-sugar-like consistency. (If using an electric grinder, do it in small short grinds to avoid getting hot.) Set it aside in a sealed box.

Once the candy bar has been frozen for a while, get it out and quickly grind it into a fine powder. It's tough to get it super fine, due to the caramel; you may need to refreeze and grind it some more. The better the grind, the better the rocket.

Once it's well powdered, mix the powdered candy bar and the powdered potassium nitrate. If using a hand grinder, feel free to grind the two together (carefully minding heat and sparks). If not, it must be mixed well with a spoon.

bar, which we found did not work as well (nearly not at all). Turns out that the higher chocolate concentration was forming too much of a charred carbon/ash and was insulating the oxidizer, keeping if from getting hot enough to work.

I had done some test burns of the Milkyway, and oxidizer, but we also wound up doing test burns with several types of chocolate bars to see if any worked better. They did not. I suspect the malted nugget is helping it act more like pure sugar.

To do the test, we would make a pile and light it with a fuse (or a torch) and see how well it burned. This is worth doing with your powder, too, before you go through the work of making the rocket. If it's popping and spitting too much, you may not have ground it finely enough or not mixed it well enough.

Step 4: Powder Testing (Optional)

I first tried Milky Way. Later, one of my co-hackers picked up the project and tried just plain milk chocolate Hershey's

Step 5: Time to Fill the Engine

Similar to the step of making the plug, we are going to add a little fuel/oxidizer, and then tamp, and then add some, and tamp. . . . Add a full teaspoon of powder mix into the PVC tube, insert the bolt, and tamp it down with 5 or so blows of the hammer. Remove the bolt and add another spoon, and tamp. Keep going until you run out of fuel, or until you are about ⁴/₅" from the top of the tube after tamping. This will be for the top plug. Mark the fuel level, fill the remaining space with powdered kitty litter, and tamp it down. You may need to fill it up a few times as each time it will compact a little less. Once it's not packing much more, you can quit.

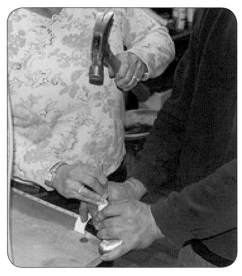

Step 6: Drilling Out the Throat and Nozzle

Using a small drill bit, 3–4 mm, drill a pilot hole through the bottom plug (this would be the first layer of kitty litter you put in the tube and has been the bottom of the engine since the start). It would be best to drill this with a drill press to make the hole nice and vertical, drilling in until you all most meet the other plug.

Be sure to remove the bit and clear out any fuel stuck in it from time to time. Also dump out any loose powder. We want this to be a very clean hole.

Now re-drill it with a bigger bit. I used about a 6 mm (I think 7 mm would be even better; you can experiment with different sizes). This hole up inside the rocket is called the throat.

And then lastly you need to create a nozzle (or a cone) by grinding away some of the plug around the throat hole. I used a ½" drill bit and just held it in my hand and twirled it to flare out the nozzle.

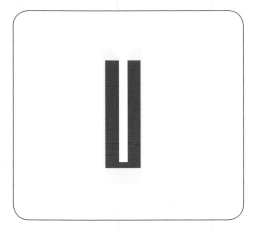

Step 7: Woosh!

It was ignited by a small bit of cannon fuse. I'm pretty sure we could have used a standard Estes rocket engine igniter, but we didn't have any on hand.

It might be a little anticlimactic, since we didn't actually put it in a rocket and launch it, or even strap a stick to it and make a big bottle rocket. But we currently have some burn restrictions here (drought), so we are keeping it on the ground for now. That will come in the future.

chemical

Eco Office Rocket: Build a Rocket from Trash

By: sshuggi
(http://www.instructables.com/
id/Eco-Office-Rocket-Build-a-
Rocket-from-Trash/)

Don't throw away those old papers. Turn them into a rocket! Whether you're just bored at work or want to have your own "space race" at the office while your boss is on vacation, the Eco Office Rocket is for you. It's a great way to kill time, recycle trash, and take a break from your day-to-day activities.

Step 1: Materials and Tools

Materials:

- At least four sheets of paper1 file folder or similar sturdy paper
- 1 plastic bag of any size
- 1 sheet of toilet paper
- 1 good rubber band
- 1 paperclip
- 1 pen

Tools:

- Ruler (print one)
- Scissors
- Tape

Step 2: Make the Body Tube

(Pictures relate to numbers.)

1. Determine what diameter of engine you want. As you may guess, the size and price are directly proportional. (C6-5s that I have were less than $10 for three.)
2.1. Do a simple $c = \pi d$ calculation to find out your body tube's inner diameter. (For A to C motors, use 56.55 mm.)
2.2. Make a straight line this distance, c, that is parallel from the edge of your paper.
3. Loosely roll the paper on itself with your line inside the roll.
4. Tighten up your tube such that the internal edge of the paper is lying along the line you made. Make sure the top and bottom are relatively flat.
5. Tape the tube in the middle.
6. Tape another sheet on the tube in line with the first. (Tape the top, bottom, and middle.)
7. Repeat this until you have a sturdy tube. (I used three sheets. For larger diameter motors, use more.)
8. Tape the last sheet in the middle, then the full length of the edge.

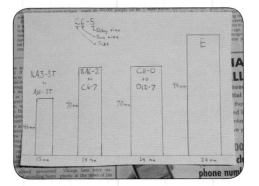

Step 3: Make the Motor Mount

(Pictures relate to numbers.)

1. Straighten out a paperclip.
2–3. Using your scissors as pliers, make a small 90° bend on one end (a little over ⅛" long).
4–5. Using the scissors again, make another 90° bend out of the other end, such that the length of your motor will fit in between. (A to C motors are 70 mm long.)
6. Make a note of where you need to insert the paperclip. You want about ¼" of the motor exposed so you can easily pull it out.)
7. Using a finger to prevent the body tube from crumpling, poke a hole through the body tube. (You may want to rough up the tip of the paperclip to make it into more of a needle.)
8. After you poke through the one side, poke through the opposite side remaining perpendicular to the body tube.
9–10. After you're through both sides, bend the remaining bit of the paperclip down.
11. Tape over the paperclip about two times.
12. Tape over the middle of the paperclip about two times. (Make sure you can still bend the bottom of the paperclip up.)

91

chemical

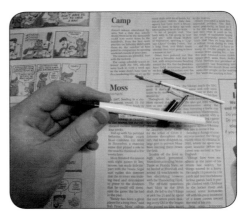

Step 4: Make the Nose Cone

(Pictures relate to numbers)

1. Disassemble your pen to just the pointy cap and the tube.
2. Cut the tube about two inches from the cap.
3. Cut long strips of paper about 1–1.5" wide.

4–5. Wrap the paper around the pen at a slight angle, starting at the cap. Loosely coil the paper at first, and then tighten to the right shape.

6–8. Add strips until it is the right diameter to fit in the body tube. (You may need to trim down the strips.)

9. Cut some half-width strip of tape. (You can easily tear them.)

10–11. Wrap them around the nose cone until you have enough to form a stop to keep the nose cone from falling into the body tube.

12–14. Wrap a long strip of tape around nose cone from the pen cap to the tape stop. (When the tape gets too high of an angle, crimp the tape and wrap over them.)

15. Gently crimp down the bottom of the nose cone so it can easily fit into the body tube.

chemical

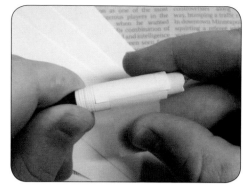

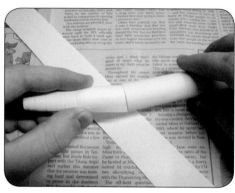

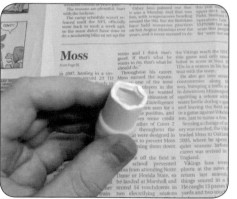

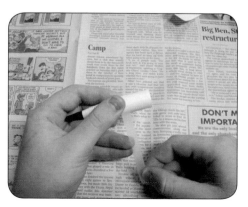

Step 5: Attaching the Nose Cone

(Pictures relate to numbers)

1. Poke a slit for your rubber band about 2" from the top. (The bottom has the motor mount.)
2. Cut your rubber band into a strip.
3. Wiggle the rubber band through your hole.

chemical

4. Cut about ½" off the end of the ink tube.

5. Knot the rubber band around the piece of the ink tube.

6. Tape the knot down into a low profile position.

7. Cut three strips of tape about 1' long.

8. Fold the tape on itself.

9. Line up the three strips and tape them onto something.

10. Braid the tape.

11. Put the right in the middle.

12. Put the left in the middle and repeat.

13–14. Tape off the ends into a tight coil.

15. Cut off the tip of the pen cap on the nose cone so the tape string can fit through.

16. Thread the string through and tie a knot to prevent it from slipping back through the hole.

17. Bend the three strips back and tape them down.

18. Tie the tape string to the rubber band.

19. Tape over the knot.

Note: The rocket tends to land on the top of the tube. It isn't going fast enough to mess it up, but add a few wraps of tape just around the top of the body tube to stiffen it up.

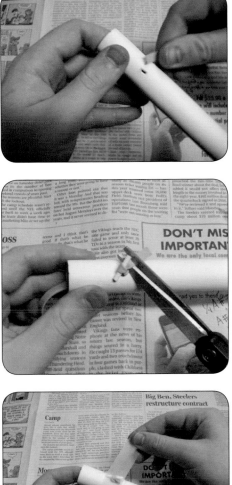

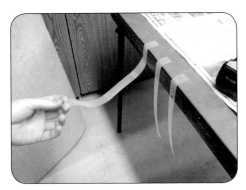

chemical

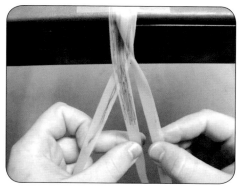

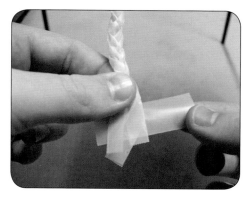

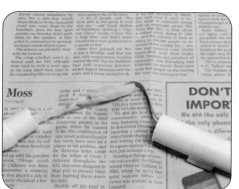

Step 6: Make the Recovery System

(Pictures relate to numbers)

1. Cut your bag into ~1" wide strips that are ~5' long. (Tie them together if you need to.)
2. Tie them onto the rubber band (maximum of two for this size motor).
3. Fold the strips.
4. Roll the strips.
5. Wad the toilet paper around the roll.
6. Insert the wad into the body tube.

Note: I chose to use streamers instead of a parachute for two reasons. One, the rocket is small and light enough that the streamers slow it well enough. Two, I am limiting myself to the tape string that is way too thick for this size body tube. If you are making a larger rocket and/or have thinner string, feel free to try and use a parachute.

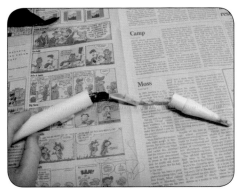

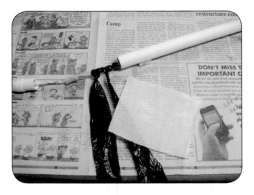

Step 7: Make the Fins

(Pictures relate to numbers)

1. Find the middle of your file folder (typically 5.75").
2. Choose a desirable fin shape. (Make the leading edge on the fold.)
3–5. Using the first fin as a guide, cut out three or four fins.
6. Cut a small slit at the top of the fins.
7. Bend out the flaps at a 90° angle to make tabs, which better stabilize the fins. (You can use a ruler/desk edge to make a clean fold.)
8. Tape down the trailing edges.
9–11. Tape the fins onto the rocket. (Avoid the motor mount; it needs to open and close.)
12. Tape the top ends of the tabs tightly.

13. Tape a couple strips around the remaining pen tube. This is called the launch lug.

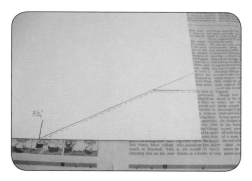

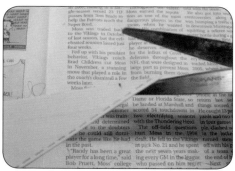

Step 8: You're Finished!

Add some color to your rocket. It'll help you see it in the sky and find it on the ground. (I went with Christmas colors because that's all I had.) Also, if your motor doesn't fit snugly in the body tube, add a wrapping of paper to snugly fit it in. You need a good seal for the ejection charge (when it blows the nose cone off and the streamers out).

I hope the build was interesting enough to get you through that boring

chemical

work day. If you still have time to kill, think about adding the following things:

A payload section: All you would have to do is make a second, wider tube and a second nose cone that goes the other way.

A parachute (for wider rockets): Plastic will work, but reinforce where you attach the string. It rips easy.

Put the fins on at an angle: It makes it fly straighter, but it's tougher to attach the fins.

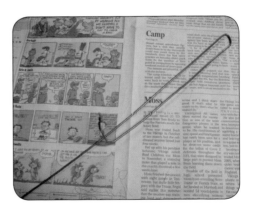

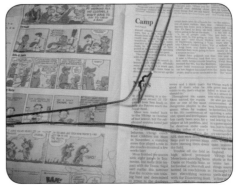

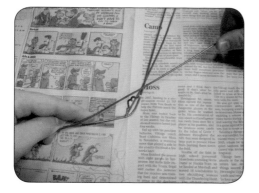

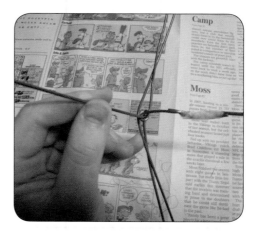

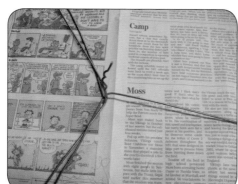

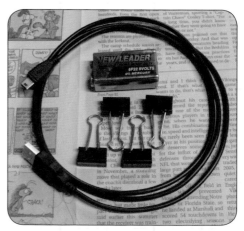

chemical

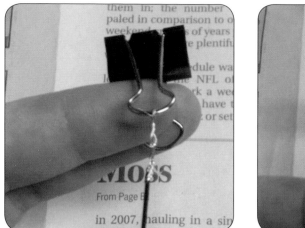

chemical

Visco Fuse Bottle Rockets

By: Dandeman321
(www.instructables.com/id/
Visco-Fuse-Bottle-Rockets/)

This Instructable will show you how to make your own bottle rockets using Visco fuse as propellant. Visco can be purchased at many online stores. I buy mine from the local firework wholesale shop. I am not taking any credit for this design, I have just modified it. The changes I've made have been mostly weight reduction. I have made changes to the bamboo skewer, the crimping method, the crimper spacer, and the amount of computer paper used. In my first test, I noticed that the rocket did not shoot straight up but off to the side. This could have been due to a few different reasons, but when I reduced the overall weight and crimped it a certain way, it seemed to fix it. This was also posted at skylighter.com as well and originated from a book written by Lancaster. Just a quick side note: I do not take any responsibility for your actions while constructing this firework or any others presented to you by myself.

Step 1: Gather the Required Materials

- 1 hot glue gun
- 1 drill with ⅛" bit
- 1 1" × 3" strip of masking tape
- 1 glue stick
- 1 2.5" length of Visco fuse 6 1" lengths of Visco fuse
- 1 1.75" × 5" strip of computer printer paper
- 1 ballpoint pen (Make sure it has a slightly rounded end.)
- 1 length of twine or string
- 1 bamboo skewer
- 1 pair of scissors
- Optional: various powdered metals, such as zinc, aluminum, or titanium

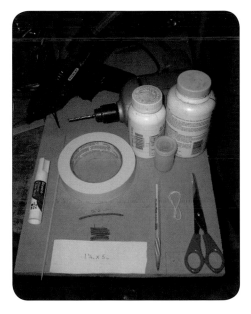

Step 2: Making the Crimping Spacer

The crimping spacer will allow you to crimp the nozzles of these rockets a whole lot easier. The original design was published in a newsletter from skylighter.com and used a wooden dowel rod. I did not have a dowel rod handy and decided a pen would work great. First, start off by measuring 1" from the end of the pen and cut it off. Next, drill a ⅛" hole into the end and make sure the fuse fits in nice and smooth. Lastly, wrap some tape ⅜" down from the end cap until it is about ¼" thick.

Step 3: Rolling the Engine

Start off by laying your 3" long piece of masking tape down on a smooth surface, sticky side up. Lay the long piece of Visco fuse ¼" from the bottom, followed by all six of the small pieces. Before you roll it up you can add some metal shavings or powder to color the tail of your rocket, but it's only optional. Start from the bottom and roll it up as tightly as you can. You want to get the long fuse in the middle, surrounded by the six smaller fuses. Usually, you will have to reposition the longer fuse to get it just right. After you have it all rolled up, lay down your computer paper strip and cover it with your glue stick. Place your fuse package about ¼" from the top. I use my crimping spacer to make sure I have enough room for the crimp (about ¼" as well). Roll it all the way up and squirt a bit of hot glue on the top to seal it. You have to make sure you have no holes for the pressure to escape, but also keep in mind that you do not want too much glue, as it will weigh down your rocket.

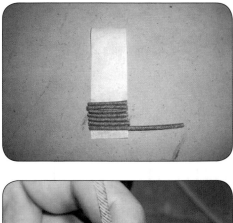

Step 4: Crimping

This step is key. If the crimp is not tight enough or is not correctly done, the rocket will just burn. It may be a bit complicated, but after you do one and see what I'm talking about, it should come easier. Start off by inserting your crimping spacer, feeding the fuse through the hole, until the masking tape stops it from entering any further. Next, feel around for the space that is created between your spacer and the bottom of your fuses and work it around and squeeze it. You want to make it weaker than the rest of the tube so it will fold easily. Now firmly grip the top of the rocket with one hand and the spacer with the other. Slowly twist and push until the paper folds down nicely. To finish it off, tie a knot around it with your string to keep it from unfolding.

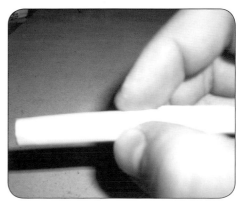

chemical

105

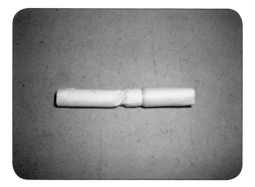

Step 5: Attaching the Guide

For this, you will need a bamboo skewer. In order to reduce the weight of the rocket, we are going to cut the skewer in half, as shown. Smear a bit of hot glue on one end and stick it to your rocket. And that's it! You're finished! I have yet to experiment with payloads and such, but I assume that you would be able to put a firecracker on top of there.

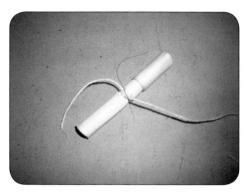

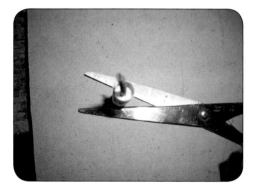

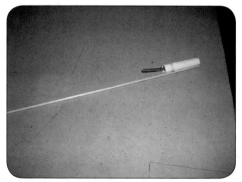

chemical

Section 5
Launchers

Handheld Rocket Launcher!

By: kaptaink_cg
(http://www.instructables.com/
id/Handheld-Rocket-Launcher/)

Back when I was in high school (early '90s), boredom inspired me to create a handheld rocket launcher out of miscellaneous parts I found in my dad's garage. It worked spectacularly . . . once. After that, I never got it operational again, and it eventually found its way back into the pile of parts. Recently I have been feeling exceedingly nostalgic and, for the past few years, I've felt the urge to create a new and improved version. So I now proudly present to you the Handheld Rocket Launcher Mk II.

Note: The legality of this item falls into a bit of a grey zone (similar to potato cannons). The state of Arizona is especially interesting, since model rockets are legal, but any type of firework or sparkler is not. *Do not* aim this at *any* living thing! Use common sense and safety if you choose to build/ use one of these! It is for educational and entertainment only, as it has no practical value at all. To put it bluntly, don't be an idiot with this thing. I'm not responsible for any accidents you may incur.

Step 1: Concept

The Launcher is powered by a 9-volt battery. The power has an illuminated safety switch and will not fire unless the switch is "armed." Pull the trigger and a current is passed through the copper barrel and a steel washer at the base of the barrel. If a properly constructed, missile is loaded at this time, it will complete the circuit, lighting the igniter and the missile will be launched from the barrel.

Step 2: Materials
- 1" diameter x 24" long copper pipe
- 1" threaded copper adapter
- 1" threaded PVC cap
- Piece of leather (optional)
- Wood, 2.5" × 24" × ¼"
- Wood screws #4, ⅝"
- #12, 2" machine bolt w/ nut (not shown)
- 18-gauge speaker wire (I also used other smaller wires as well)
- Insulated ring terminal (two different sizes)
- 2 fender washers, ⅛" × ¾"
- Momentary contact push button
- Illuminated toggle switch
- 9-volt clip
- 1" insulated clamps
- Steel rivet, ⅛" diameter x ½" grip

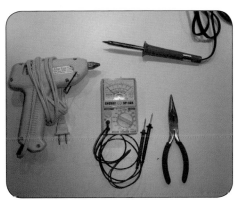

Step 3: Tools

- Drill
- Jigsaw
- Miscellaneous drill bits (including ½" and 1") (not shown)
- Screwdriver
- Dremel (equired for virtually *every* project)
- Needle-nose pliers
- Wire strippers
- Torch
- Rivet tool (What's the proper name for this?)
- Soldering iron (optional but recommended)
- Ohmmeter (optional but recommended)
- Hot glue gun (optional but recommended)

Step 4: Copper Work

Solder the copper fitting to the pipe. It's recommended to coat the end of the pipe and the inside of the fitting with flux prior to soldering. It helps the solder flow into the joint. Using the torch, heat the fitting (not the pipe itself). Once hot enough, the solder will melt and be sucked into the joint. Wipe it down with a rag and let it cool.

launchers

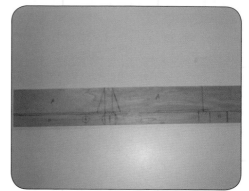

Step 5: Wood Cutting

Using the supplied schematic at the end of this Instructable, mark out the pieces onto the wood as shown. Start by cutting the strip with B, C, and D off. I used a jigsaw, but a table saw would have been much better for this step. Cut out pieces A and B next. To create a perfect curved end to B and C, clamp them to a working surface, and then drill out the circle using a 1" bit. Do not drill the holes for the buttons yet!

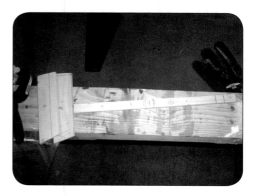

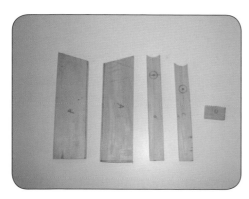

launchers

Step 6: Handle Construction

Mark out the locations of the button holes and ends on the wood pieces. You will need these lines to locate the holes for the screws. Be sure to stagger the holes in such a way that ensures they don't enter any of the button holes, and they won't hit each other. I went a bit overboard with the holes. You'll see in photos of the final product that I didn't need this many. Use your own discretion on this step.

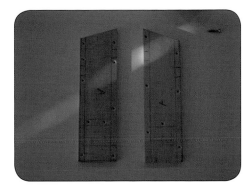

Since the heads of the screws have a taper on them, we'll need to countersink the holes a bit. If we don't, there is a good chance the screws will split the wood. I used a small boring bit on the Dremel to create the countersinks.

Assemble the handle. Be sure to use pilot holes for the screws so that the wood does not split! Drill the button holes using a ½" bit, keeping them as centered as possible. I decided on a whim to stain the handle. Definitely not required but adds to the "cool factor" (an important quality in all of my instructables).

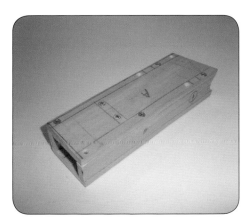

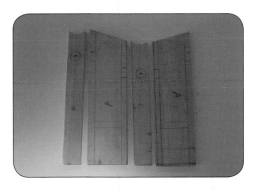

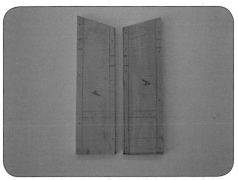

Step 7: Handle Attachment

For me, this was the most difficult part of the build. Take your time on this step. Take the two 1" clamps, and if yours are insulated, remove the insulation. Bend them so both legs are at equal lengths. Next, position them over the barrel and onto the handle in such a way that the bracket will hold the handle flush. Drill a $7/32$" hole through the handle. It will have to be located so as to miss both switches. On my prototype it was a little bit loose, and I had to resort to using the hot glue gun to keep the handle from slipping around on the barrel.

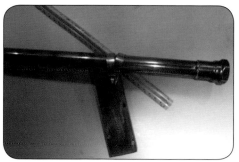

Step 8: Ignition System

Open up the handle and install the electronics per the attached schematic. Make sure the threads on your buttons are long enough to penetrate the wood. I almost had to countersink my trigger! When you have it put together, pull the speaker wire almost all of the way apart. Cut the positive lead to just a few inches long and attach a ring terminal large enough to go over the #12 bolt. The negative lead should be about 16" long. Once wired up, it is recommended you test the system using your ohmmeter. Set it to 10V DC test and connect it to the end terminals. You need to verify there is *only* a charge when both the safety switch is on *and* the trigger is pushed. This is a very important step. You do not want this thing firing unexpectedly. The safety switch should illuminate when it's "armed."

To eliminate the possibility of a short, I filled the button terminals with hot glue. Next, scuff up the top of the battery clip and, using wood glue, attach it to piece D. I used cellophane tape to secure it in place while the glue dried.

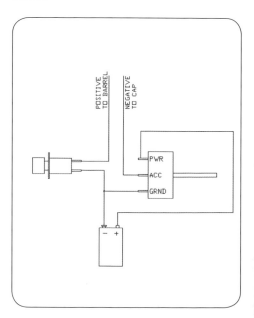

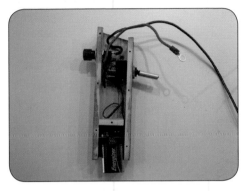

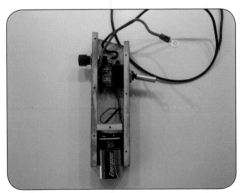

and taping it to the end of the barrel. Start each port with an ⅛" hole, and then enlarge to a ³/₁₆" bit. Do not apply too much pressure with the drill or you could deform the barrel.

After the holes are drilled, take your Dremel or a file, and spend the time to make the inside of the barrel smooth again. If it's not smooth enough the fins of the missile might get caught. Not pretty.

Step 9: Barrel Porting

I chose to "port" the barrel for a couple of reasons. First it (hypothetically) will reduce turbulence for the missile by allowing the gases to escape from the sides of the barrel instead of competing for room at the mouth of the barrel. Other than that, it looks rather cool, and I'm anticipating short flames/smoke shooting from them ("cool factor").

Begin by printing the template provided at the end of this Instructable

Step 10: Handle Attachment

With the handle reassembled, cut a small notch in the arch above the safety switch with your Dremel. Lay the wires in this notch and then attach the handle to the barrel with your 1" clamps and bolt. Slip the positive lead ring terminal over the bolt. Wrap the negative lead around the barrel a few times and cut to the desired length. Attach the smaller ring terminal to the negative lead.

I had planned on ripping the card stock out but the rivet gripped too hard and I never got it out. Perhaps if I had put the card stock on the other side of the washer it would have worked better.

After this step is complete, get out your ohmmeter again. Set it to 10V DC and touch the positive probe to the barrel and the negative to the inside washer on the PVC cap. Verify that you are getting 9-volts when the trigger is pulled.

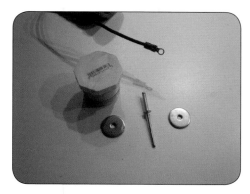

Step 11: End Cap Construction and Testing

Drill a ⅛" hole in the cap. Widen it slightly. Starting from the outside, the rivet should pass through the ring terminal, a washer, a piece of card stock (more on that in a second), through the cap, and then secure the second washer inside the cap.

The card stock was a good idea that didn't work well at all. I wanted the ring terminal to be able to spin on the rivet.

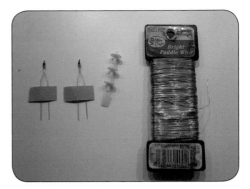

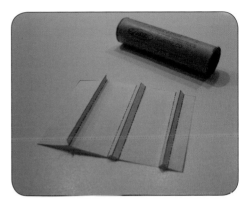

Step 12: Missile Construction
Materials needed:

- Pack of rocket engines (with igniters and plugs)
- Printed templates from the end of this Instructable
- Thin conductive tying wire

Any standard size rocket engine will work. I had some B4-4s lying around that I used. The ideal rocket would be a C engine used for glider rockets. These have no ejection charge, so they have a better power to weight ratio.

Cut out the fins and nosecone templates. Bend the fins in a series of peaks and valleys as shown. Wrap and glue around the top of the rocket engine. These cannot go at the bottom of the rocket or it will not sit properly inside the PVC cap. Next, cut out and glue the nosecones on as shown.

Install the igniter as you normally would using the plastic plug. Remove the tape holding the leads together. Bend one lead up the side of the rocket. Twist the other lead into a coil-spring. These leads *must not touch* or it will not fire. Cut a piece of tying wire and loop it against the straight lead, securing it in place with a small piece of tape. This tying wire must bend outward as shown to ensure it makes contact with the copper barrel.

launchers

115

Step 13: Launch Aftermath

It works, but the rockets weren't nearly as stable as I had hoped. Perhaps using different strength engines would help, or creating a longer missile by taping a used engine to the front of a fresh engine. Weighting the nose cone could also be beneficial.

The escaping gases actually stung my hand a little bit.

The rocket has to be cleaned out at least a little between shots. If there is too much residue in the barrel, the ignition wires can't pick up the current.

launchers

116

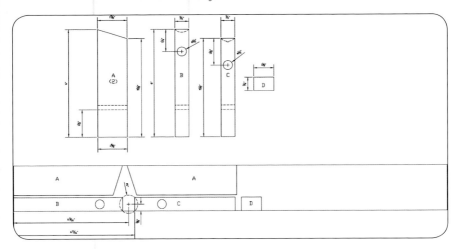

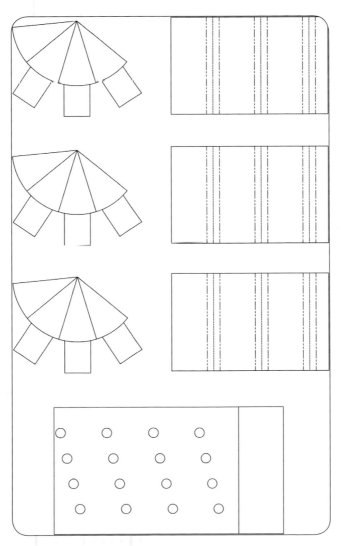

One-Hundred-Yard Paper Rocket Launcher

By: WYE_Lance
(http://www.instructables.com/
id/100-Yard-Paper-Rocket-
Launcher/)

PVC paper rocket launcher designs are a dime-a-dozen. So why another one? Because I've tried many other designs found on Google and YouTube, and none of them are fairly easy to build, perform spectacularly, or are easy for kids to operate. I have finally come up with a design that fulfills all the criteria for an amazing rocket launcher, after conducting the paper rocket project with my engineering class countless times.

This Instructable also outlines how to make a high-performing rocket, which is just as important as having a great launcher. The students in my engineering class have made rockets that can fly over 100 yards from this launcher—it's rather mind-blowing to witness.

Step 1: Make the Launcher

I work with elementary-school aged children, so making the launcher is something I do as part of my prep. Older kids (with a generous budget) can try to design their own launcher. View the last step for a complete list of materials.

This launcher works up to 60 PSI. You can wire in a second 9-volt battery to get the launcher up to 100 PSI. Sixty PSI is enough to achieve spectacular results. Pressures above that dramatically increase the risk of exploding the rocket, and, in my experience, most student-built rockets cannot withstand the speeds produced by more than 70 PSI.

By the way, you might want to protect your work surface a bit better than I did.

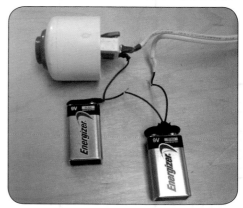

118

Step 2: Make the Rocket

- Card stock
- Tape
- Scissors

It's easy to build a rocket that can reach a distance of 50'. However, making an ultra-high-performing rocket is actually quite challenging, because all aspects need to be designed to near perfection. At high speeds, tiny imperfections are quickly blown out of proportion because the forces acting upon the rocket are intensified. For example, a nose cone that leans slightly to one side may not significantly influence the rocket's performance at 40 PSI. However, at 60 PSI, that nose cone may create an imbalance of friction created by the air rushing by, causing the rocket to turn sharply and tumble to the ground.

For this reason, take your time while creating and attaching each part of the rocket. And with that in mind, here's how to make a high-performing rocket

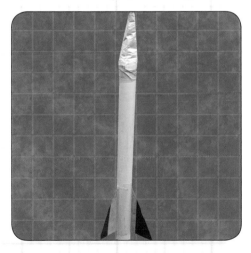

Step 3: The Lesson (for Teachers)

Learning Objective

- Fundamental concepts in aerodynamics such as stability, drag, and propulsion are experientially explored and applied as students build and test their rockets. The comprehension of these concepts is further strengthened as students redesign and retest their rockets while observing the differences in performance.
- Students will acknowledge the value of teamwork as they work in pairs to design and build their rocket.
- Students who choose to work individually will quickly observe the value of teamwork during certain steps.
- Basic rocket anatomy vocabulary (fuselage, fins, and nose cone) will be understood and utilized during the teacher's lecture and during rocket construction.
- Fine motor skills are developed during rocket construction.
- Optional: Students will experientially comprehend the values of different materials as they apply their material choices to their rocket design, as well as by observing the performance of different material combinations.

Lesson Plan

I usually start by explaining how the launcher works because it catches the students' attention right away. I just explain the basics: The chamber is filled with air, creating high air pressure, and when the button is pressed, the air is allowed to escape through the launch tube, which provides propulsion to the rockets.

Next, I show the class how to build a rocket from start to finish. I usually work a little fast and imprecisely since I'm just outlining the steps, so be sure to encourage them to take their time and build with precision. As I build the rocket, I explain the important aspects of each part:

The fuselage must fit the ½" PVC perfectly. If it is too tight, it will not

launchers

119

fit, or it will explode upon launch. If it's too loose, propulsion (pressurized air) will escape out from the bottom of the rocket. The fuselage should slide onto the launch tube with little wiggle room.

The fins provide stability for the rocket—this is enough explanation for younger students. Older students may benefit from knowing this: When a rocket is pushed off course by a gust of wind, the angle of attack (direction the air is moving) relative to the fins changes, which causes the fins to generate a small amount of lift. The lift immediately forces the rocket to return to its original trajectory, which also restores the angle of attack to 0, thus stabilizing the rocket. If the fins are too large or not straight, it may generate too much lift and cause the rocket to turn during flight. If a rocket begins to turn because of the fins, the center of pressure (the point at which all forces are acting upon the rocket, including momentum and lift) surpasses the center of gravity, meaning the rocket will try to turn around, causing it to tumble out of control. Basically, make your fins precisely and tape them on straight!

The nose cone reduces drag (air pushing against all sides of the rocket) by offering minimum aerodynamic resistance. In other words, the nosecone helps the rocket "push" its way through the air without allowing the air to push back against the tip of the rocket, instead flowing smoothly around it. Demonstrate how to build the nose cone a few times since it can be challenging. The nose cone can be difficult for young students to build, so an alternative (though less effective) design is to simply pinch the end of the rocket and close it with tape. Be sure to tell the students to secure their nose cone extremely well because the air pressure can blow the cone off of the rocket.

Inspect each part of the rocket for straightness and secure placement.

I also encourage the students to work in pairs for this project for two reasons. Firstly, it is simply easier to construct a rocket if one person holds the parts in position while the other secures it with tape; secondly, flaws in the rocket design are more easily identified and resolved when two people are examining the design and expressing their thoughts and ideas.

Remember, the objective is to allow students to explore and comprehend aerospace ideas experientially, so allow them to experiment with different rocket lengths, nose cone and fin shapes, number of fins, etc. It's okay if students cannot give you a textbook definition of ideas like drag and trajectory at the end of class. As long as they are engaged with the activity, they will learn these things effortlessly.

Alternative Ideas

You can offer a myriad of materials for the students to explore and build with, which adds a new dimension to the project. Experimenting with different materials can add longevity to the lesson.

Step 4: Safety, Tips, and Troubleshooting

Follow these safety precautions regardless of whether the chamber is pressurized or loaded with a rocket.

- Never allow students to use the launcher unsupervised. Disable the launcher by removing the battery (or pump or launch tube) if you have to leave the launcher unsupervised.
- Never allow anyone to put their face near the launch tube. Air expelled from the tube, if forced into someone's nose or mouth, is powerful enough to cause the lungs to rupture. This is very serious. Tell your students about this and they will be frightened enough to never

launchers

get near the tip of the launch tube.

- Never stand directly in front of the launcher, even if a rocket is not loaded. At point blank, a rocket shot from the launcher can cause serious injury.
- The student holding the button should keep his/her trigger finger off of the button until the final countdown is initiated. The button is sensitive and can easily misfire.
- Use a bright rope to define a safety zone that the students may never cross, even while loading their rocket.
- Have a countdown before each launch as a way to alert people in the area (and to make each launch more exciting!).

Common Design Flaws

- Fins that are not attached straight, or if the leading tip of the fin is not secured, will cause the rocket to tumble at high speeds.
- Fins that are too big create too much lift and/or drag.
- Fins that are too small may not provide enough stability.
- Fins that extend too far from the fuselage are prone to wobbling in the wind, causing instability.
- Nose cones that are not secured well enough will explode off of the rocket.

Tips and Troubleshooting

Rockets tend to explode at pressures above 60 PSI. If you choose to mod the button with a second 9-volt battery, have the students tape up every seam many times over.

Inspect the rocket before each flight and use your hands to straighten out the fins and nose cone, which will inevitably become bent over time.

I usually refrain from interfering with students' designs. However, if a student has created a poorly built fuselage I will

step in and help them. Making a new fuselage after attaching everything else can be a hassle.

Young students (grades three and below) may have a hard time rolling a tube of card stock, so I usually do that step as part of my prep.

If you don't have access to a huge open space, you can set up targets like stacked cardboard boxes and aim for those. Be extra cautious here.

When storing the launcher, remove the 9-volt battery, or at least make sure the button is uncompressed, or else the battery will quickly drain.

Step 5: Materials List

Here's the complete list of materials and tools for the launcher and paper rockets.

Tools for the air pressure chamber

- Sandpaper
- PVC cutting tool
- Drill
- Mallet
- Pipe wrench
- Latex gloves

Materials for the air pressure chamber

- PVC primer
- PVC solvent weld (aka PVC cement)
- KwikPlastic (or similar)
- Tire valve
- 2 6" sections of 2-inch PVC

launchers

121

- 2 2" slip fit end cap
- 2" slip fit T-joints
- 2" to 1" slip fit reducer
- 2" section of 1" PVC
- 2 1" threaded male adapter
- 1" to ½" slip fit reducer
- 24" piece of ½" PVC with tapered end
- Modified valve and replacement launch handle from ItsaBlast.com
- Bicycle pump with PSI gauge

For the base
- 12" cable ties
- 2 PVC elbow joints
- 2 12" piece of PVC with two holes drilled about 4" apart
- 8" piece of PVC

For paper rockets
- Card stock
- Masking tape
- Scissors

The total cost is about $70, excluding all tools and solvent weld. In my line of work, it is well worth the initial investment because the paper rocket activity is very cheap—less than $0.15 per student.

Pocket Rocket Launcher

By: zjharva

(http://www.instructables.com/
id/Pocket-Rocket-Launcher/)

This is a real rocket launcher that fits in your pocket. It is easy and cheap!

Step 1: Parts and Tools

Almost all of these can be bought at Radioshack.

Materials

- Altoids' tin
- DPDT Heavy Duty Rocker Switch
- Mini SPST Momentary Push Button Switch
- Red LED with holder And built-in resistor
- 9-volt battery snap
- 9-volt battery
- 9/16" wide copper tubing (can be found at Radioshack)
- Alligator clip
- Test leads
- Wire A10-3T or A10-PT rocket engines (available at Hobbytown)

Tools

- Wire strippers
- Pliers
- Metal snippers
- Pocket knife
- Soldering iron
- Hot glue gun
- Pipe cutter
- Drill
- Large drill bits
- Small drill bit
- Block of wood
- Clamp

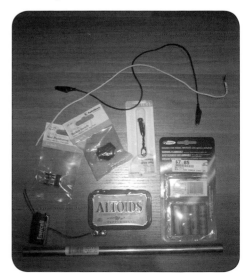

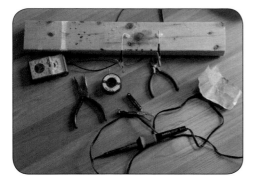

Step 2: Getting the Tin Ready

This step involves creating holes for the rocket and switches to go through.

Parts and Tools

- Altoids' tin
- Pliers
- Metal snippers
- Drill
- Large drill bits
- A small drill bit
- Round file
- Clamp
- Wood block

Bend the metal tabs holding the lid on back. Remove the lid. Bend one tab so that there is no hole in the tin. Then, bend one tab so it is flat against the tin (picture 1). Cut off the bottom metal on one of the holes on the lid (picture 2). Mark the size of the holes for the switch and tubing. Put a block of wood in the tin and clamp it down. This makes the tin not bend. Drill them out. If the holes aren't big enough, file them out (picture 3, 4, 5, and 6). Drill a hole in the back for the LED using previous techniques (picture 7). Shave off some of the screw on ring of the rocker switch (picture 8). Cut an approximately 3" piece of pipe. If the pipe cutter made an indent on the pipe, file it out (pictures 9 and 10). Check and see if everything fits (picture 11).

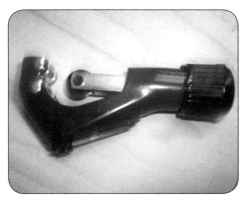

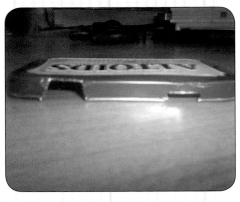

launchers

together. Be sure to slip on shrink wrap before you solder it. Then shrink the shrink wrap (pictures 1 and 2). Solder the red wire from the battery snap to one of the tabs on it. Be sure to shrink wrap it. Then, solder a short piece of wire to the other tab (pictures 3, 4, and 5). Solder the red wire from the LED, a short piece of wire, and the wire from the rocker switch together. Shrink wrap it all with the short piece of wire sticking out back towards the switch (picture 6; disregard the color of the wire, it was just some salvaged wire). Solder the short piece of wire to one of the tabs on the momentary switch, and shrink wrap it. Solder the other alligator clip to the other tab of the momentary switch and shrink wrap it (pictures 7 and 8). When you turn the rocker switch on, the back LED should light up. If the alligator clips are touching and you press the momentary switch, the LED should go out (picture 9).

Step 3: Solder It

This is the step when you solder the switches.

Parts and Tools

- Rocker switch
- Push momentary switch
- LED
- 9-volt battery snap
- Soldering iron
- Solder
- Wire
- Wire stripper

Cut the alligator clips in half so you have two alligator clips with wires. Solder the battery snap's black wire, the LED's black wire, and one alligator clip

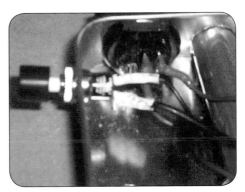

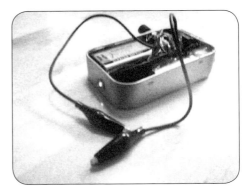

Step 4: Finishing Touches

For the finishing touches you need:

- Hot glue gun
- Hot glue sticks
- Soda can
- Scissors
- Metal snips
- Electrical tape (optional)
- Scissors

Measure and cut a piece of soda can metal the length and height of the tin, with a notch big enough for the wires

launchers

to go through. Cover with tape for a "stealthy" look. This is the blast shield (picture 1). Glue all of the solder points and wires down, except for the alligator clips and the battery snap. Also, glue the blast shield and launch tube (picture 2). Cut out a slot on top for the rocker switch so you can close it all the way (pictures 3 and 4).

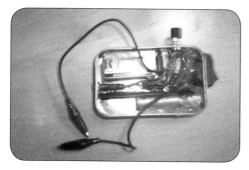

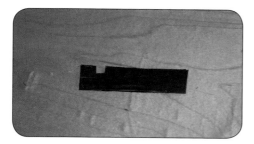

Step 5: Launching!

This is what you need to launch it:

- The assembled launcher
- Rocket motor
- Rocket igniter
- Ignitor plug
- Gloves
- Common sense

Insert the igniter, plug into the rocket, and slide down the tube. Connect the alligator clips. Put on your gloves and turn on the rocker switch. Make sure the LED comes on (picture 1). Use your brain and common sense. Point away from people, pets, and flammable things. Press the button. After a little delay and a puff of smoke, off it goes (picture 2)!

launchers

In this Instructable, I will demonstrate how I built a launching pad for a water rocket and, at the same time, how I built my first water rocket. When building it, I paid attention to safety for my kids (the bottle can be painful on face), and I was focused on building a launching pad with materials found in the woodshed and garage of a country house:

- 2 wooden pieces, 10 cm × 10 cm
- 1 wooden piece, 15 cm × 1.8 cm
- 1 easel

The measures are approximate; they depend on materials that you will find in your garage. The important thing is the final result: The launching pad must force the rocket to follow a trajectory.

launchers

Step 2: Build Rocket

You must be sure that the cork completely seals the bottle, otherwise you must put tape around the circumference of the cork. The plug must be longer than the cork. Make a hole in the cork for the plug (make it very tight).

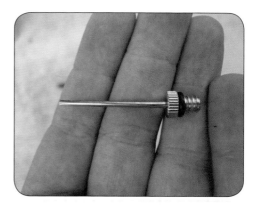

Step 1: Materials and Tools

- Plastic bottle
- Electrical tape
- Bottle cork
- Cutter
- Scissors
- Air pump
- Soccer ball plug valve
- And a drill

131

Step 3: Launch

Don't put too much water in the bottle (see the photos). Push the cork very strong in the nozzle of the bottle. Put the rocket on the launching pad and pump the air and lift off!

Section 6
Extra Special Rockets

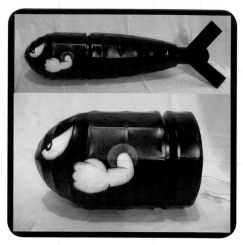

Bullet Bill is a character that has appeared as an enemy in almost all of the Super Mario games from the very beginning. There are a few varieties, and their look and behavior has changed over the years. Like me, I'm sure you've been killed by a Bullet Bill many times.

I enjoy making crazy, non-traditional model rockets. I built regular ones as a kid, and I still find it extremely rewarding to test out new building methods and to push what I can do with simple, inexpensive materials.

I thought it would be neat to build a life-size Bullet Bill model rocket, as it provided all sorts of great challenges. I ended up building two versions, both of which I thought were beautiful in many ways, and they taught me a lot of new tricks.

Version one is covered briefly in Steps 1–3. I began this first attempt with most of the planning focused on how to create a lightweight, visually accurate model of Bullet Bill. I didn't think much about its flight-worthiness until it was complete. At that point, I knew it surely wouldn't fly well, but thought, "Well, let's just go shoot this off and see what happens."

It didn't end pretty.

For version two, which the photos show here, I applied the building techniques I learned with version one but paid closer attention to giving it a shot at actually flying. It was scaled down a bit, and built (somewhat) more like a real model rocket.

special

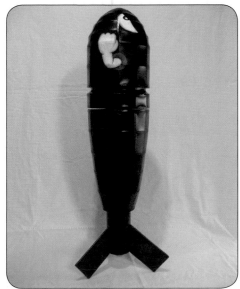

Step 1: Version One—A Quick View

This is a quick view of version one. Both versions were built from:

- Foam core
- Card stock
- Thin painters' masking paper
- A lot of glue

Version one was 19" tall and 12" in diameter (without the fins attached). Construction details were very similar for both versions, and will be covered fully in Steps 4–14.

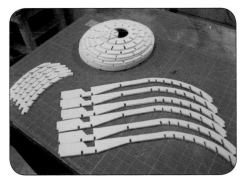

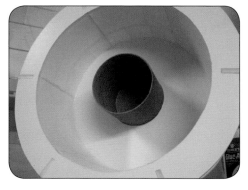

Step 2: Version One—Finished Details

I was quite proud of the finished result of this rocket and was tempted to not even shoot it off, knowing the likely consequence.

For both versions, the launch rod goes directly through the middle of the rocket, and a cluster engine setup is used.

special

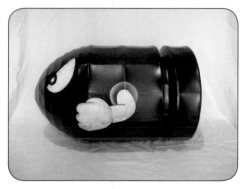

Step 3: Version One—Launch

I launched this off of a small cliff with the hopes that the extra space below would allow a little more time for the chute to open. No such luck.

Step 4: Version Two—Homemade Rocket Tube

After all the work for version one and the awful launch, I was surprised at how quickly I wanted to get back to this. I couldn't go down like that!

I began version two by making a homemade paper tube. I've been making my own rocket tubes for a few years, and I'll be honest—it's tricky and can be messy and frustrating. But it is very rewarding to make your own lightweight rocket tubes.

I figured out this method through a lot of trial and error. I found that using a straight piece of PVC works best as a blank. I cut out strips of brown craft paper and roll one tightly onto the blank. This is taped in place at the ends of the paper strip, making sure the edges of the strip don't overlap each other and the entire strip sits snugly on the tube.

A second strip is painted with white glue (or wood glue) that has been watered down, about one part water to four parts glue. This is carefully rolled over the first strip, being sure to cover the seams. Three or four layers of craft paper can be done, although for this I only did two. Each layer needs to be quickly rolled and pressed into place. The paper is extremely porous and the glue bonds the paper almost immediately, so you only get one chance. I've tried all sorts of other adhesives, and only white and wood glue have worked for me.

A final layer is added in the same manner, except using painters' masking paper instead. This type of paper is thinner and less porous than the craft paper, and makes finishing much better. It is sealed with a coating of the watered-down glue, and then lightly sanded with 220-grit sandpaper.

The paper tube is cut from the PVC and is slid off to dry. If you spread the glue thinly and evenly, and don't stretch the paper too much, the tube will dry straight. If not, you'll have a warped and worthless tube, which I have made a lot of!

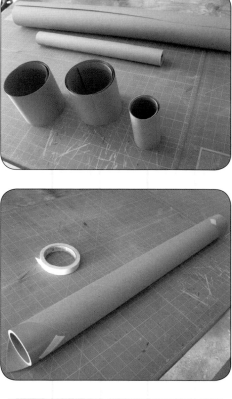

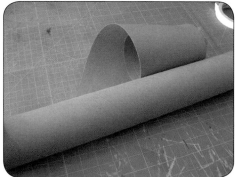

special

Step 5: Engine Mounts and Fins

The engine mounts were made using foam core and store-bought tubes that fit the size engines I was using (D- and E-size).

Fins were made with ¼" balsa. When gluing things like wood and paper, it's always best to put a thin layer on both surfaces, wait a few seconds, and then put them together. Once each fin was dry, fillets were added with more glue.

The most useful tools for this project were a circular protractor for laying out angles, scientific calculator for figuring radii and such, metric rulers, X-acto blades, cutting mats, and a couple of good compasses.

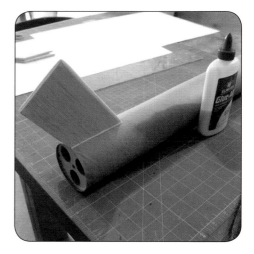

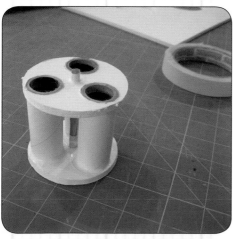

Step 6: Bullet Bill Nose Cone

In version two, Bullet Bill is the nose cone. This was made with a skeleton of foam core, just like version one. The design was laid out on paper, carefully cut out with X-acto blades, and pieced together like a puzzle. This was all glued with regular white glue. Once the glue was dried, I used a sharp utility blade to shave off the square edges of the circular pieces on the dome.

If you're interested in making something like this, there are scans of the plan I made for version two at the end of this Instructable. The plan may not be precisely the same size as my original once you print it out and piece it together, but it should help you get going.

If you just want to make a lightweight model of the Bullet Bill character, it should work well for you. Cut out the cross section-piece and use it as a stencil to trace and cut out six pieces from foam core. Match a compass up to the plans to determine the various distances needed to lay out the circle pieces. Use a protractor to lay out where the notches will go to fit the cross pieces. Study these pictures carefully to see what you need to do. It will be challenging, but you'll get it!

special

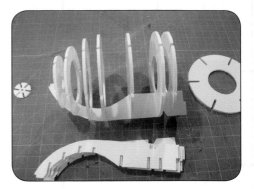

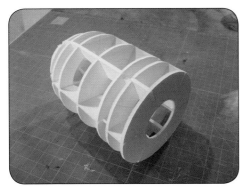

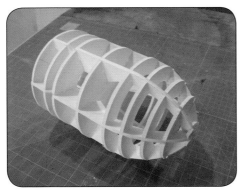

Step 7: Nose Cone to Tube Transition

The bottom of the nose cone had to receive the top of the tube snugly, but not too tightly. This should, in theory, pop off when it's time for the parachute to come out and bring the rocket safely back to the ground.

This area was made with light card stock.

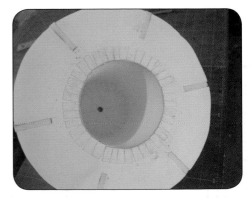

special

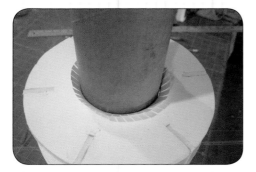

Step 9: Covering

I found that painters' masking paper is a great covering for this type of model. Each piece of covering is cut out separately, painted entirely with watered-down glue, and quickly glued in place. As the glue-wash dries, the piece of covering stretches and becomes tight.

A light coating of glue over the entire surface helps strengthen the covering.

Step 8: Bullet Ridge

The ridge on the bullet was made with pieces of card stock that were carefully measured, cut out, and glued in place.

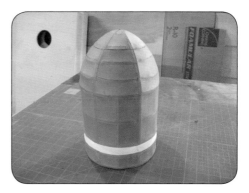

Step 10: Rocket Body

The rocket body was made of foam core that was built directly onto the tube and covered in the same manner as the nose cone.

Step 11: Painting

A few coats of primer were used to seal up the paper and make it ready for the final coat of paint. The rocket was painted with two coats of flat black spray paint.

Step 12: Details

I made some stencils to help me lay out the details for the rocket. The details were painted on with craft paint, and the rocket received a light coat of lacquer to seal it up and make everything shine.

Step 13: Parachute

The parachute was made from rip-stop nylon. I hit the edges with just a touch of flame to melt them and keep them from fraying.

Step 14: Launch Preparation

I did some balance tests and determined that I needed to add about 2 oz to the nose to make this flight-worthy. I cut out one of the panels on the nose, added the right amount weight,

special

and patched it up. The final flight-ready weight was just a little over one.

The parachute, wadding, and nose cone had to be prepared for launch with the launch rod in place. Three D-size engines were used.

The launch pad is homemade, and the launch controller is a modified Estes cheap-o that I hook up to my cordless drill battery. For cluster engine launches, I have an octopus-like attachment that works very well.

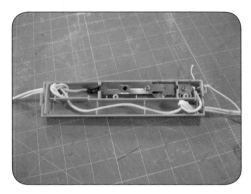

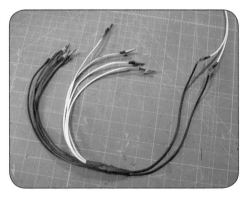

Step 56: Final Thoughts

Bullet Bill version two's flight was fantastic. The rocket flew straight, and it flew high.

The parachute failure just killed me, though. It was due to a stupid, avoidable oversight in the design. When the chute deployed, it went straight into the nose cone, and there it stayed. If I had built a paper cylinder of some kind inside the back of the nose cone, it would have prevented the chute from being shot up inside of it

special

and getting stuck. You can basically see what happened in pictures 4 and 5.

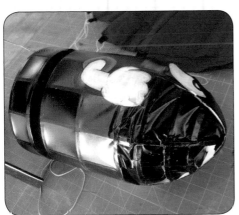

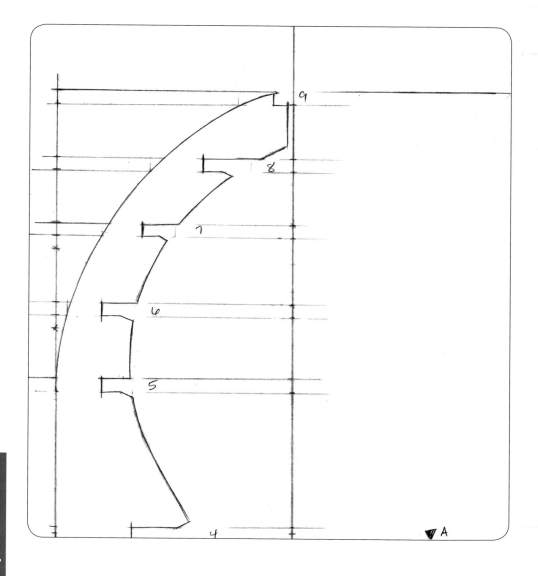

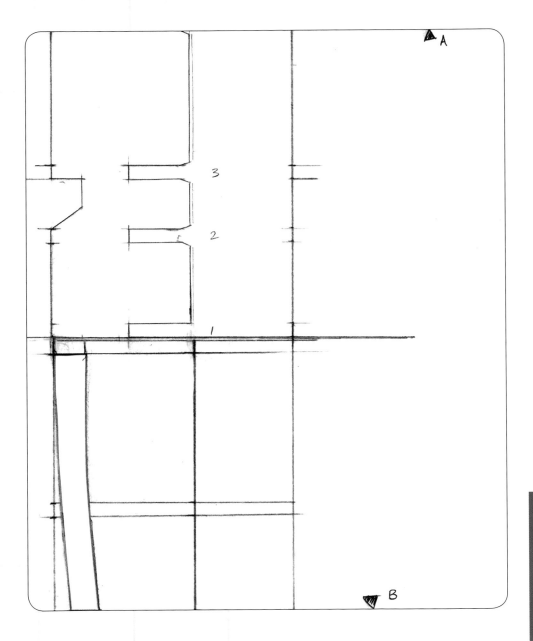

special

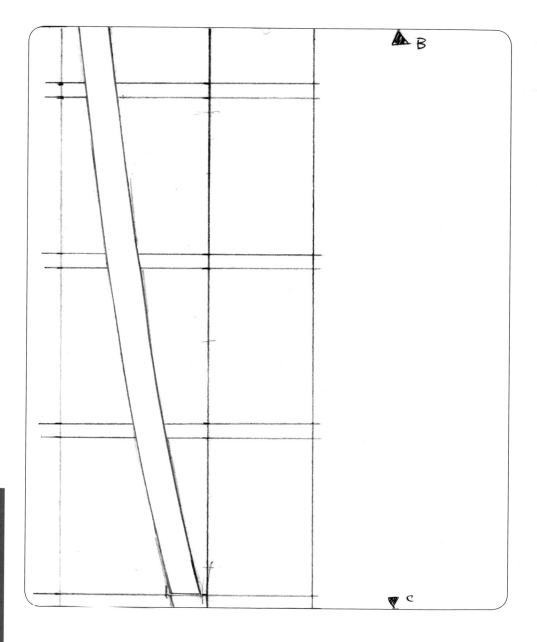

B

C

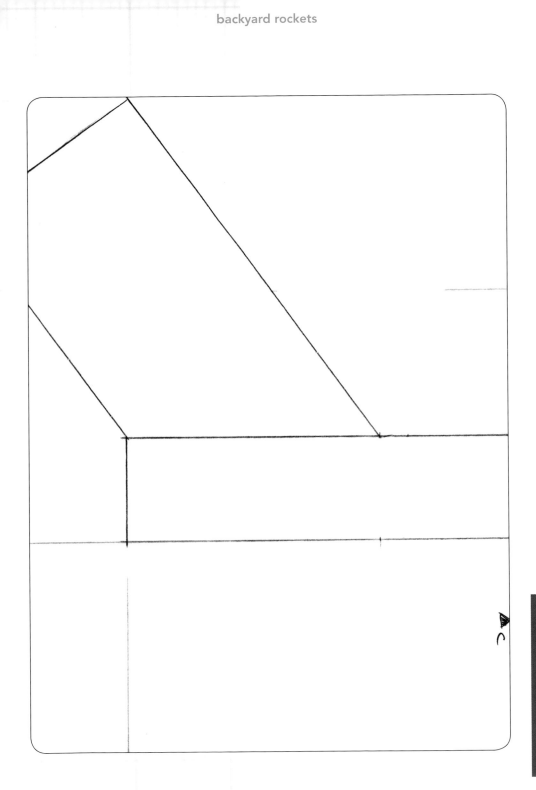

This is a completely scratch-built model rocket designed to carry my GoPro camera. It is 42" tall, flies on three "E" size Estes motors, and it's recovered by a 54" parachute. The camera is housed completely within the main body tube (not in the nose cone), which allows for great footage on the way up and great right-side-up footage on the way down. This also eliminates any drag issues.

Step 1: Rocket Body Tubes

Two 18" tubes were made using the method I have outlined in this Instructable (http://www.instructables.com/id/Make-your-own-Kraft-Paper-Tubes/). Each tube was made using a 3" mailing tube as a blank.

Step 2: Motor Housing

The motor housing tubes were made using the same method described in the previous step. The engine block rings shown in the first photo were made from ¼" MDF. The two circles that hold the three motor tubes were cut from ⅛" craft plywood. All craft plywood used for this project was cut with a scroll saw.

Step 3: Connect Two Body Tubes

The motor housing was glued in place in the end of one of the body tubes. I removed 2.5" from each tube, one to be used as a coupling and the other to be used as part of the camera housing. Pieces of craft plywood were cut and glued into the tubes to act as reinforcement.

Step 4: Fins

Four fins were made from ³⁄₁₆" balsa. These were glued in place with wood glue. These were made extra large to create enough drag so the rocket will fly stable.

Step 5: Camera Housing

The camera housing was made with craft plywood along with the body tube material that was removed earlier on. Scrap foam was cut to shape and glued in place to hold the camera snug within the housing.

special

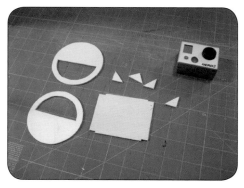

Step 6: Add Camera Housing to Body Tube

An opening was cut in the body tube where the camera bay will be exposed. The camera housing unit was slid in from the top of the tube and glued in place.

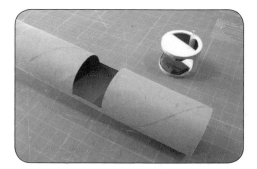

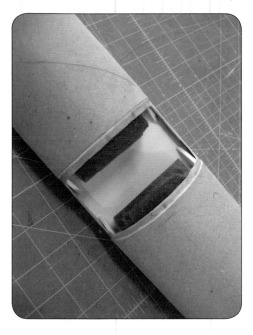

Step 7: Nose Cone

This part was the highlight of the project for me. I've always struggled with making my own nose cones for homemade model rockets, and I finally found a method that produced something I was mostly happy with. It will take some refining, but it worked reasonably well this first time around.

The nose cone was made from 1" pink foam insulation circles that were cut, glued together, and then shaped on a homemade makeshift lathe. I used a sanding block with 60-grit sandpaper to sand down the foam into the final nose cone shape.

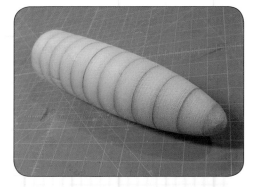

Step 8: Parachute

The parachute was made with polyester jacket liner and tulle. I was hesitant to make a parachute in this manner for a model rocket, as both materials are fairly flammable. If the parachute is packed properly and an appropriate amount of wadding is used, it should be fine.

Step 9: Paint

The nose cone was painted with three coats of decoupage gloss to seal it prior to painting with spray paint. (Spray paint eats the foam if it is not sealed well.) The entire rocket received a few coats of primer and then three coats of white spray paint.

special

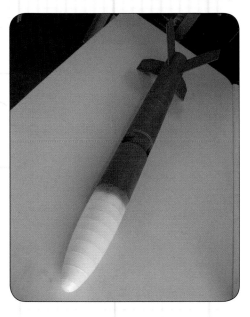

once the camera is turned on and placed in the bay in preparation for flight. I'm excited to get some great shots with it. Watch out neighbors!

Step 10: Camera Bay Cover

The camera bay is covered by a piece of plastic cut from a 1-liter soda bottle. It is taped in place with clear tape

Iron Man Model Rocket

By: seamster
(http://www.instructables.com/
id/Iron-Man-Model-Rocket/)

Instructable that details what I did: http://www.instructables.com/id/Hand-carved-Iron-Man-head/.

I have loved model rockets since I was a kid; but, instead of building from kits, I prefer to make funky ones from scratch. About a year ago, I got the idea to make a dual-engine model rocket in the shape of Iron Man. The idea presented a lot of unique challenges—which I've enjoyed working on—but this was one project I was happy to finally get out of the way.

I spent many nights lying awake trying to figure out how to make a man-shaped model rocket flight-stable, how and what to make him out of (to keep the weight down), how to construct the parachute deployment system, how to mount him onto a launch rod, what kind of launcher I would have to make, and on and on. I resolved most of the issues, and I'll show you how all of these ideas came together.

There were plenty of missteps and failures along the way throughout this project, but I've cut most of that out in order to keep this as straight-forward as possible. Please excuse the shoddiness of the exterior details on the finished rocket. This is less about the actual Iron Man character, and more about my journey and the process of trying to make and fly a crazy man-shaped rocket. In the end, you'll see that I had mixed results with this project.

I began by making the head, which I figured would be the hardest part. You can design your own head, buy something fitting from a store, or, if you're really into this, see my separate

156

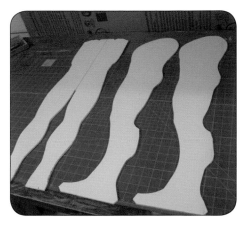

Step 1: Body

I laid out a design for the body by copying details from photos of Iron Man and an Iron Man toy I borrowed from a friend. If you're feeling ambitious, I've included illustrations with the front and side lay-outs that I created at the end of this Instructable. The total height of the finished rocket is 36".

I ordered rocket supplies from apogeerockets.com, which has been a very nice company to work with. I ordered a bunch of 24 mm tubes (which hold D- and E-size Estes model rocket engines), some tube couplers, engine block rings, launch lugs, and kevlar cord.

My first attempt at making the body was with layers of pink insulation foam glued together, with the rocket tube structure sandwiched inside. I used a sharp knife to carve out the body shape, which was tedious and messy. In the end it weighed too much to use and I had miscalculated the proportions, so the head which I had already finished was too small for the body. After plenty of cursing, the pink foam body ended up in the trash . . . in very tiny pieces. I re-sized the lay-out, and waited a few months till I was ready to work on it again.

For my second attempt, I decided to build the body up using foam board (¼" foam sandwiched between paper). This proved to work very nicely for making a lightweight skeletal-type structure, but led to some difficulties in covering.

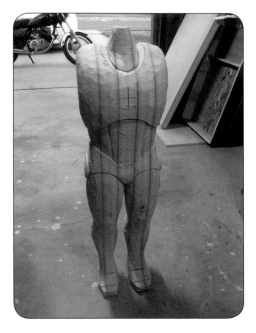

Step 2: Rocket Tube Structure

The rocket tube structure was assembled with regular white glue. The 45° cuts were made using a miter saw.

The parachute deployment system I came up with is basically a hatch attached to the back of the rocket with a long cord that is shot off when the engines backfire. The parachute is attached to the cord, but is stored in a compartment all its own outside of the actual rocket tubes. This is a technique I've used on other oddball rockets and it seems to work well, if I make sure there is no way for the parachute to get stuck once the hatch is blown out of the way.

Step 3: Exhaust Tube

The two main tubes lead to one exhaust tube. Prior to gluing, surfaces of the tubes were roughened up with sandpaper.

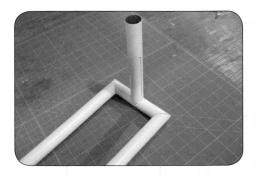

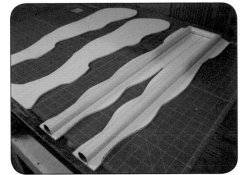

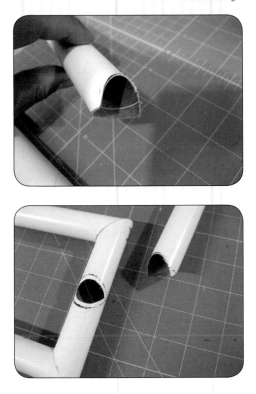

Step 4: Building Up the Body

The foam board body cross-sections were glued to the rocket tubes to build up the body. White glue was used for this. Notice the slight space left at the bottom of the tubes where the foot pieces were added.

There was a lot of shaping, reshaping, and moving things around from this point on. This was very much a sculpture, and required quite a bit of eyeballing and continually adjusting things to suit my tastes.

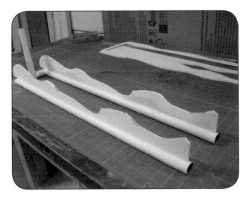

Step 5: The Launcher

Before I got too far on the body, I had to figure out how this was going to be launched, and where to put the launch lugs (the little tubes that hold the rocket to the launch rod to guide the rocket on take-off).

I paused here and built a launcher, and figured out how to have the rod go right up through the middle of the rocket without coming out the top of Iron Man's head. This launcher design

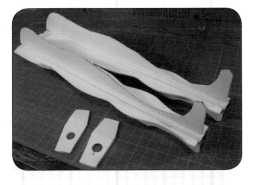

special

159

was made specifically to accommodate some giant removable fins I was going place underneath Iron Man's feet when it was time to fly. These were going to be added to increase flight stability.

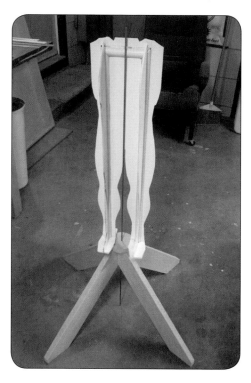

Step 6: Finishing Up the Skeletal Structure

I made individually shaped pieces out of foam board to fill-out and define the body. I tried lots of things prior to this, but this method seemed to produce the lightest, most effective results. These pieces were all glued on with hot glue. This step required some modifying to the body cross sections to get a shape I was ultimately satisfied with.

I've included a couple of photos of some failed tries at finishing the body. For various reasons, neither idea worked very well.

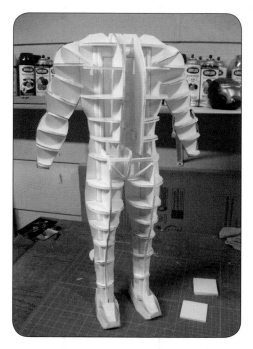

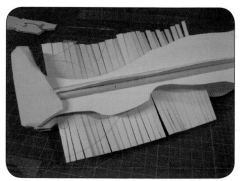

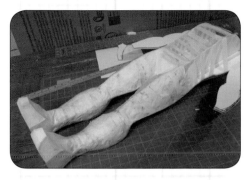

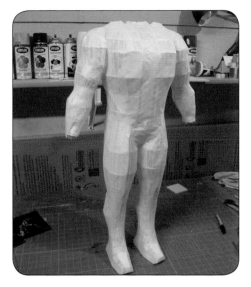

Step 8: Craft Foam Covering

I probably should have just painted the tape and called it good. But I thought it would look nice to give him a clean covering of craft foam. I cut individual pieces to fit and used 3M 77 spray adhesive to glue them in place. I thought the legs turned out looking pretty slick. But I realized how dumb it was to add this extra weight to a thing that was probably going to crash, so I didn't completely finish covering the body with the craft foam.

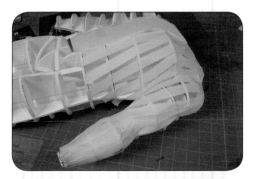

Step 7: A Layer of Skin

I used masking tape to create a skin over the body shape. This took two rolls of tape, and added quite a bit of weight.

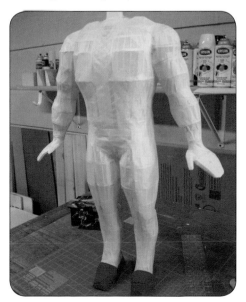

special

161

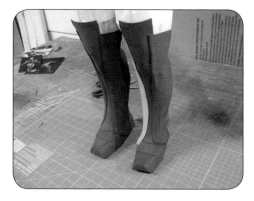

followed with a few spots of gold and a spot of white. I used a thick permanent marker to draw in some details, and glued the head in place.

Even though it seemed like I was trying to make this look crappy, it still turned out decent . . . if you're squinting from about 10' away.

Step 9: Painting

I'm pretty good with a spray can, and I prefer Krylon, specifically because of the adjustable fan-spray nozzle that they started using in the last few years. It helps you make nice, even coats, and that's the key to a nice paint job.

However, this is not a good example of my spray skills, or the niceness of Krylon paint, for which I apologize. This was a messy, heavy, primerless single coat of crimson red, immediately

special

Step 10: Launch

I couldn't wait to launch this to see what would happen. I didn't even put a parachute in it, which actually negates the whole point of calling this a "model rocket" (and violates the model rocketry code . . . *cough*), but I figured it wouldn't go that high anyway. It ended up weighing so much that I wondered if it would even get off the launch pad.

I used two E engines, and went to a place way out in the middle of a dirt field away from buildings and anything flammable. I was secretly hoping for a spectacular, fiery crash.

It only went up 50 feet or so. I still thought it was pretty cool.

Step 11: Flight damage

The rough, parachute-less landing broke his neck. That was about it. (Luckily, he missed my car.)

I was surprised at how he flew. If I had made and attached some giant fins extending below his feet, I'm sure he would have flown much straighter. Still, excessive weight is the real issue I would have to overcome if I ever revisited this project.

Since the initial launch, I have removed the head piece and all the tape covering to examine some things. I found that the rocket tubes had blown out at the 45° angles near the shoulders.

That's another problem that will need to be re-designed around if I were to revisit this project. Overall however, aside from this and his head, he was in pretty good shape for the crash landing he took.

At times this was a real pain, but I had fun with it. I learned a lot of new tricks and got the satisfaction of overcoming some interesting creative challenges.

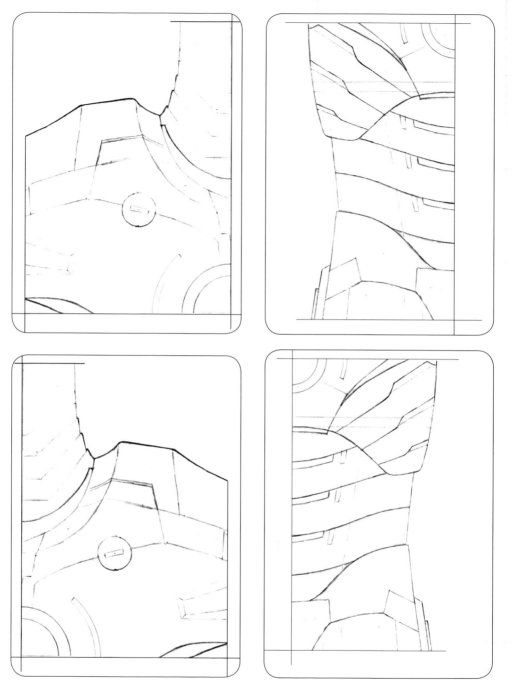

Note: You can use a copier to scale up these designs to actual size.

special

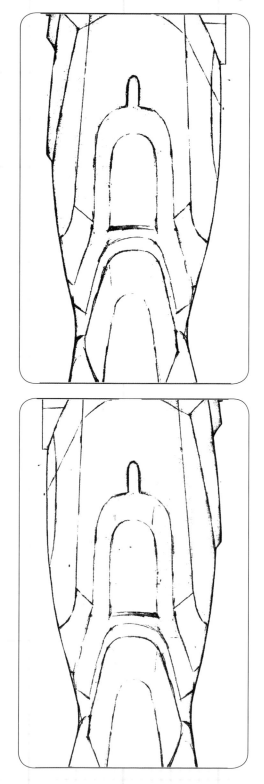
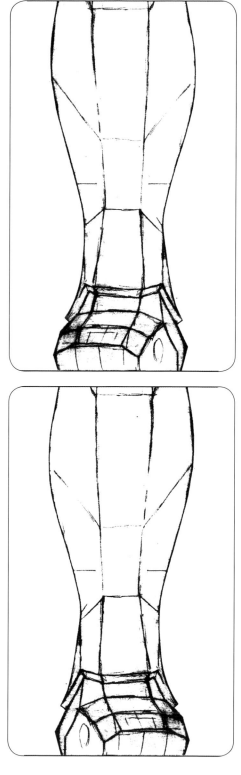

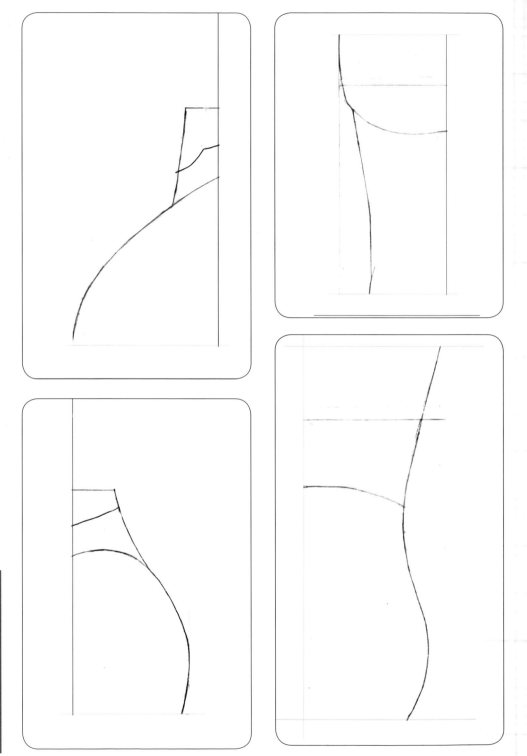

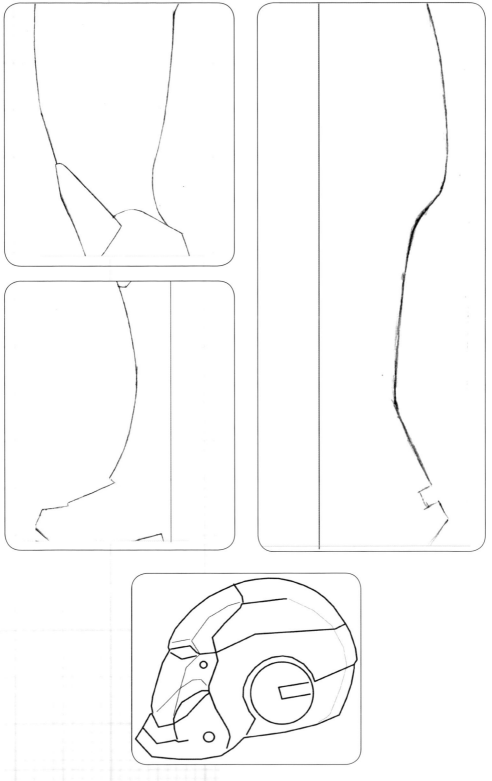

special

Mercury Joe: Semi-Scale Flying GI Joe Redstone Rocket

By: JamieClay
(http://www.instructables.com/id/Mercury-Joe-semi-scale-GI-Joe-Redstone-Rocket/)

This project was inspired forty years ago when I got a GI Joe Mercury Capsule for my birthday. I always imagined it flying (even orbiting) and it kept me out of my parent's hair for days on end. Fast-forward to the mid-1990s when the GI Joe Capsules are re-issued by Toys-"R"-Us—naturally I picked up one (well three). After the popularity and success of the Gumby flights, I simply had to look to the shelf above my workstation to be inspired for my next big project. When I found a tube that was 9.25" (the exact diameter of the Capsule base), this project was set into motion.

A lot of this project was engineered on the fly and by no means reflects the best way to approach the tasks described. It's just how I did it; you're welcome to make changes in any way that suits your engineering skills.

I offer this in hopes that this Instructable will inspire others to build and fly similar projects.

Step 1: Preamble

To send a full GI Joe capsule aloft (with astronaut), have the capsule free-fall and deploy its recovery system safely. The entire flight will be recorded by three (to five) different on-board video systems.

This is *not* a scale project; the mercury booster is a little thicker than the real thing. The mercury capsule, built from the GI Joe unit, is under scale as well.

The big challenge of this project is to perfect a system that allows the capsule to free-fall to a safe altitude before deploying its parachutes. Technically this is no more than a dual deployment flight, but the added complication of extracting the tower so the capsule can free-fall is anything but simple.

At apogee, the capsule (with tower) will decouple from the booster. The capsule has a deployment bag attached to the heat shield, which will pull out the pilot chute for the booster. The decoupling activates an ejection charge timer inside the tower, allowing for the capsule and tower to drift away from the booster, which will be unfurling its main chute. Once the tower charge has fired and its chute has inflated, the weight of the capsule causes it to fall free off the tower base. The capsule free-falls to about 1500' before deploying a pilot and main chute combination.

Step 2: Basic Design Concepts

There are three sections of the rocket that will recover via their own parachute: tower, capsule, and booster. Each section has its own avionics, video capture, and recovery system.

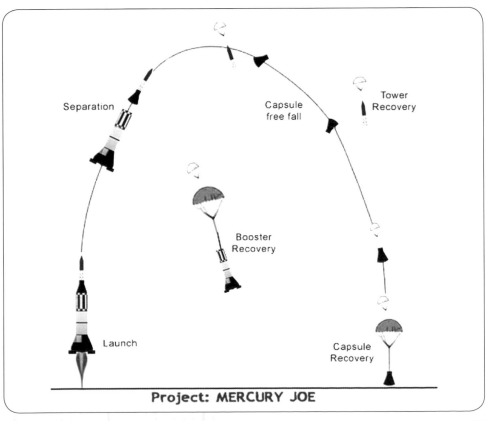

Separation

Capsule free fall

Tower Recovery

Booster Recovery

Launch

Capsule Recovery

Project: MERCURY JOE

special

The booster section is divided into two parts to make it easier to transport and store in the off season. It is held together by turnbuckles on nylon straps with a hat clip onto large eye bolts.

The capsule is fitted with a PVC end cap that couples to a ½" PVC pipe that extends down the center of the main recovery chamber. This reduces the need for a large ejection charge to blow the capsule off and push out the booster's parachute. Four centering blocks keep the capsule aligned with the body tube.

The capsule and booster have flight computers that are setup to trigger the primary decoupling at apogee. The capsule's flight computer then waits for a designated period of time (or altitude drop) before it deploys the capsule's recovery system.

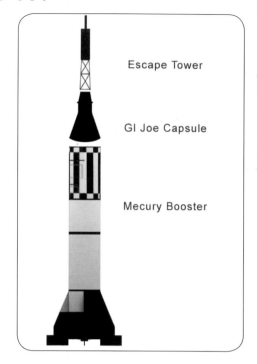

Escape Tower

GI Joe Capsule

Mecury Booster

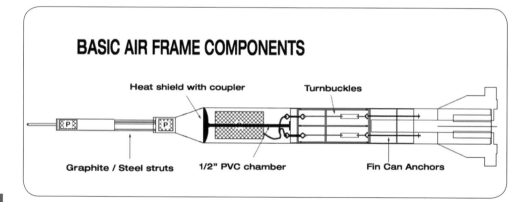

BASIC AIR FRAME COMPONENTS

Heat shield with coupler

Turnbuckles

Graphite / Steel struts

1/2" PVC chamber

Fin Can Anchors

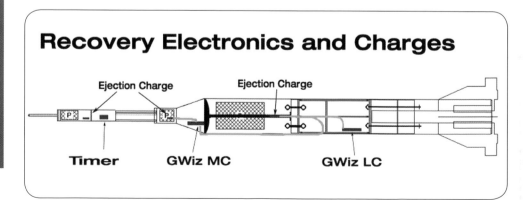

Recovery Electronics and Charges

Ejection Charge

Ejection Charge

Timer

GWiz MC

GWiz LC

special

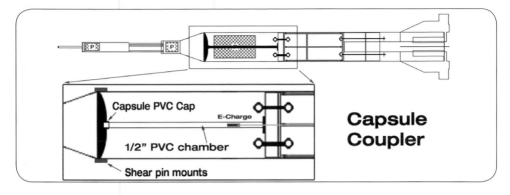

Capsule PVC Cap

E-Charge

1/2" PVC chamber

Shear pin mounts

Capsule Coupler

Step 3: The Upper Airframe

The tubing is a 9.25" Shockwave airframe tubing that comes from RDS. To give it added strength, I gave it a light coating of epoxy. This lathe is made of mounted 2" × 4"s with 1.125" holes and a 6' length of 1" gas pipe with 9.25" plywood disks. To keep the disks in place, I'll often just add tape to give them a nice friction fit.

I use a BBQ rotisserie motor, and slowly rotate the tube while I apply an even coat of the resin. Later, to aid in the sanding, I switch the rotisserie motor out with the upper head of a drill press; this gives me nice speed and torque.

Note: When sanding, I use furniture clamps to hold the lathe posts in place on the table.

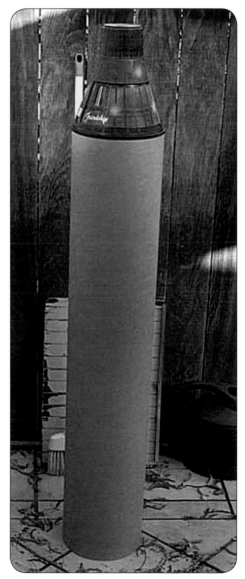

special

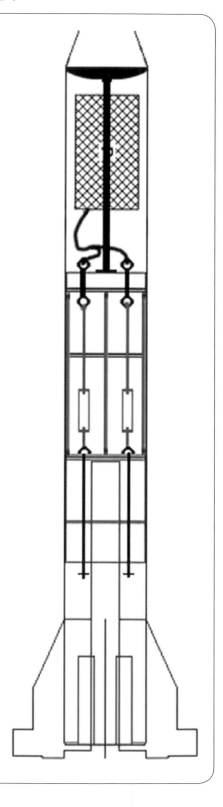

special

Step 4: The Fin Can

The fins are made of Aerospace Composite material that is edged with hardwood for added strength. You can put any motor configuration into your fin can. I decided to go with a central 75mm with four 38mm in case I want to do a cluster launch. The fin can air frame is 26" long with a 6" coupling shoulder.

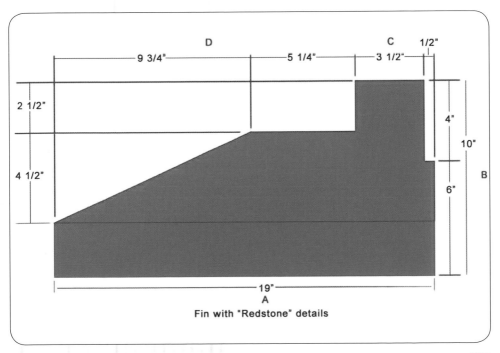

Fin with "Redstone" details

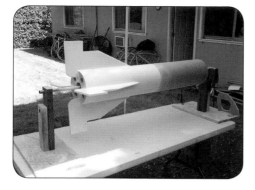

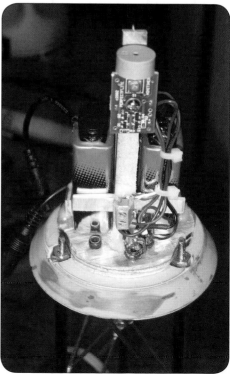

Step 5: Tower

I've actually built a few different towers and have had the best success with this variation. The important aspect about the tower is it needs to sit firmly on top of the capsule but separate once the weight of the capsule is applied.

special

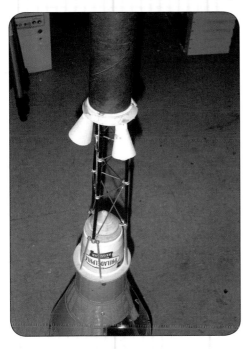

Step 6: Capsule

After following the capsule deconstruction guide, the following pictures give you an idea ofhow to reinforce the capsule for flight. After as many flights, the capsule has endured many a harsh landing, but as a testimony to the original, it helps.

The one change I made that isn't shown (well) here was that I built a fiberglass extension to the capsule nose. I used a 3.5" phenolic tube and built an end cap out of model aircraft plywood.

The Annual GI Joe convention requested Mercury Joe to make an appearance, so I shipped him off and included a demonstration video to help them better understand some of the technical aspects of the modified capsule.

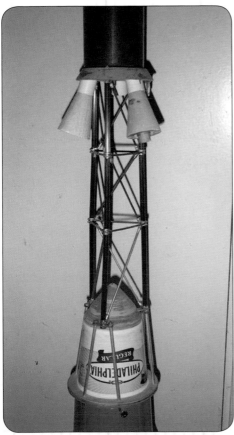

special

Step 7: Paint and Decals

Because this is a semi scale project, you don't have to get crazy getting the decals to scale but the overall look should be thematically correct.

The first time I built this project, I painted the checker pattern at the top of the Redstone; the second time, I built the pattern in Adobe Illustrator and then sent it to a decal manufacturer to make. I'm not convinced that made the job easier, as putting on such a large decal has its challenges as well. It did help to put the tube on the tube lathe, but even with that the alignment wasn't perfect. But no one really notices that sort of thing when the bird is on the pad or in the air.

I chose to paint the capsule blue instead of black, mostly because it made it more Navy-like and Alan Shepard was an Annapolis Grad (and I'm from Annapolis). Plus, the capsule isn't to scale so I felt I could take the liberty. All the lettering and flag decal came from a local arts and craft store and the black striping is automotive pin stripe. Because this is such a popular rocket to model, it's very easy to find visual references via Google.

Step 8: Flying and Recovery

If you think any component of what I've lightly described is complicated, consider that preparing this project for launch is even more so. It can take a couple hours to build the ejection charges, test the avionics batteries, make sure all the chutes are packed correctly, make sure the cameras are charged and have plenty of memory available, get the motor built and secured, and, of course, the Astronaut is well rested and ready to fly.

I highly recommend a check list; it can reduce the risk of failure considerably (but not entirely).

This rocket has flown up to 1 mile high on an M, but my preferred altitude is 2500' using an L. This allows the spectators a good clear view of all the processes working.

Flying to 2500' also makes it extremely difficult to lose sight of the three sections and, because we fly with AeroPAC out at the Black Rock desert, it's REALLY hard to lose anything, even when the smallest component manages to break free (like the cap to the capsule).

That said, when it works, all that effort is it is worth the celebration and the accolades people often shower upon you!

special

special

Step 9: Part Sources, Pages, and Suggestions

The capsule: Very often I get asked where one can buy a Hasbro GI Joe capsule. The answer is always the same: eBay. In the ten years since I started this project, I've never had a problem finding a suitable capsule and usually for less than $50.

The body tube and bulkheads: This is harder to find, yet it is key to making this particular rocket. Rocket Dynamic Systems (RDS) sells a 9.25" body tube that is the diameter of the base of the capsule. Now, if you wanted a more scale Redstone booster, you could use a 9" body tube; with the real Mercury Redstone, the capsule extended out slightly beyond the booster's diameter (see picture).

The fin material: The fins are made of Aerospace Composite material from Giant Leap Rocketry.

Avionics: You will no doubt want to use a flight computer you're familiar with. In this project, I use gear from:

- Adept—altimeter in the capsule
- PerfectFlite—timer in the tower
- GWiz—altimeter in the booster

Cameras: Over the course of this project, I've used so many different cameras, but right now the combination I like is:

- Tower Camera—BoosterVision Gearcam
- Cockpit Camera—Grayson Hobby's Aerial Cam (Note: you can also find similar ones on eBay called "Gum Stick cameras.")
- Booster Camera—Aiptek 60 fps HD camera

I also use a couple keychain cameras for additional views, like looking up the booster.

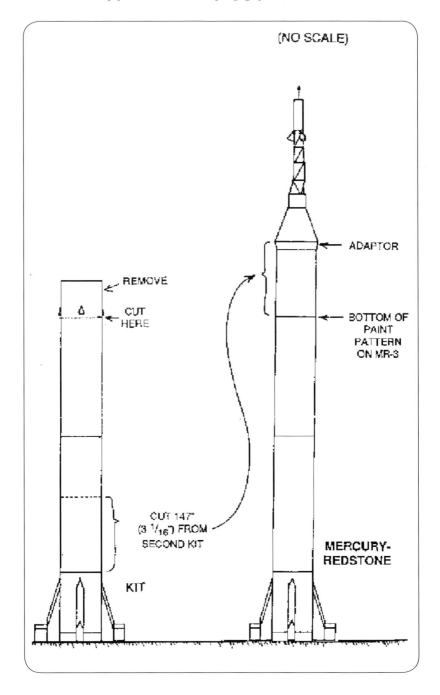

(NO SCALE)

REMOVE

CUT
HERE

Δ

CUT 147"
(3 1/16") FROM
SECOND KIT

KIT

ADAPTOR

BOTTOM OF
PAINT
PATTERN
ON MR-3

MERCURY-
REDSTONE

Model Rocket with Horizontal HD Video Keychain Camera

By: boot2skull
(http://www.instructables.com/
id/Model-Rocket-with-horizontal-
HD-video-keychain-cam/)

This is an Instructable for modifying a model rocket with a payload bay to carry a keychain HD video camera horizontally (pointing out) instead of vertically (pointing down). I decided to take on this project after seeing many cool videos of rockets with on-board video cameras that tended to face the camera downward. That is a great view, but I wanted to see what a video would look like with a camera facing horizontally.

This Instructable assumes you know the basics of building and launching model rockets. It is easy to learn and get started. I've skipped the steps of building the rocket, as those steps will follow the instructions included with the rocket aside from the rocket parts involved with this Instructable.

Note: Substitutions can be made for the model rocket being used or the keychain camera model, but doing so may alter these steps. If you change anything, be prepared to perform slightly different modifications to get your camera to fit properly. Research never hurts either.

Items Needed

Model rocket: For this Instructable, I used an Estes Reflector since it has a payload bay. I also did extensive research to make sure the payload bay

diameter (1.33") was wide enough to hold the keychain camera 1.26" wide without case).

Note: I upgraded my parachute to a larger spare 18" chute we had laying around to slow the rocket descent with the camera on board. This increased the time it takes for the rocket to come down and could be problematic in a small launch area if wind is present. The stock parachute should be fine with camera on board.

Keychain camera: Most keychain cameras will fit as you will have to remove the case. For my purposes, I selected a $30 model with true 720p HD video. I purchased it from eBay. Some camera models "claim" to have 720p or better HD video, but they actually convert lower quality video up to HD video, so do your research on other models. Also be mindful of the frame rate. Mine has a 30 fps (frames per second) frame rate, which isn't bad for such a small HD camera. Some cameras only do 15 fps which I would find unacceptable for something as fast as a rocket launch. Look for 30 fps or better.

Video Editing Software: There are plenty of free options on the internet. I used Windows Movie Maker.

Memory Card: Micro SD. Class 4 or better to handle the volume of HD video data. I used 4 gb capacity. A USB card reader will make your life easier as well.

Foam Ear plugs: A pair or more. These are for securing the camera in the payload bay, not for your ears!

Tools for Constructing the Rocket)

Consult your manual for a more complete list.

- Glue (Elmer's or other strong general purpose glue)
- Sandpaper, preferably a sanding block
- Ruler
- X-acto knife
- Spray paint—however you wish to paint your rocket. I used flat black and metallic gold.

special

- Masking tape
- Pinstriping tape—optional but it makes cleaner, more uniform paint stripes than masking tape.

Tools for Modifying the Rocket

- A saw (I used a hacksaw.)
- Glue (Elmer's or other strong general purpose glue)
- Sandpaper, preferably a sanding block
- X-acto knife
- Small, sharp kitchen knife
- Dremel—to cut a nice hole for the camera lens. An X-acto knife could probably be used instead if a Dremel is not available.
- Pen or pencil
- Small Phillips head screw driver, like the type for eye glasses.

Step 1: Notes on Rocket Selection

The rocket I used is the Estes Reflector. I selected this rocket for several reasons:

1. It has a payload bay for carrying objects. This is perfect for putting a keychain camera inside and carrying it safely. You cannot put a camera inside the body of a rocket, as this space is needed for the parachute and recovery wadding to protect the parachute. The engine's discharge to deploy the parachute travels through the body, so it needs to remain clear and unobstructed. The camera would get fried from the discharge.

2. The payload bay on the Reflector has a diameter capable of carrying the keychain camera. This is important because we shouldn't have parts of the camera (other than the lens) protruding outside the rocket. Several other model rockets with payload bays have a smaller diameter that would not fit the camera.

3. The Reflector's parts are made of wood and cardboard, which makes them very easy to modify.

Other model rockets with payload bays may yield different results. Do research if you decide to use something other than the Estes Reflector. Other model rockets may use plastic parts or require different measurements and modifications for the camera to fit.

Step 2: Build Your Rocket (Mostly)

This tutorial is made under the assumption you can build a model rocket. Most kits are not difficult. The Estes Reflector is good for beginners.

Following the instructions that came with your rocket, build the rocket, but leave all the pieces of the payload bay untouched and unfinished. These pieces include: nose cone (top), payload bay tube, and payload bay base (bottom). These parts will need to be modified to accommodate the keychain camera first. Do not attach the eye screw to the base of the payload bay. I attached the eye screw when I built my rocket, but it will save you some trouble if you attach the eye screw after the modifications are complete. Also, do not paint anything yet.

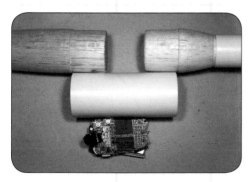

Step 3: Disassemble the Keychain Camera

We don't need the keychain case that the camera comes in. It adds unnecessary size and weight. Using a small screwdriver, remove the screws on the case. Pry the case apart and remove both halves of the case and the plastic buttons. Save these if you ever want to use the camera with the case. You may wish to tape the camera in the case to the side of a rocket to record downward facing rocket flight videos.

The camera sensor and lens may be glued to the circuit board as mine was. If so, use an X-acto knife or a small sharp kitchen knife to cut through the glue. It is the same glue used in glue guns and is relatively soft. It will take some effort and patience to cut through the glue to separate the lens/sensor assembly.

For this step, be extremely careful not to break or cut into the ribbon cable that connects the camera to the circuit board. Damaging this ribbon cable will basically ruin the camera, and these cables cannot be easily repaired as conventional soldering melts them. I'm not responsible if you damage your camera.

Once you are finished, you should have a bare camera with a sensor/lens assembly that is now movable.

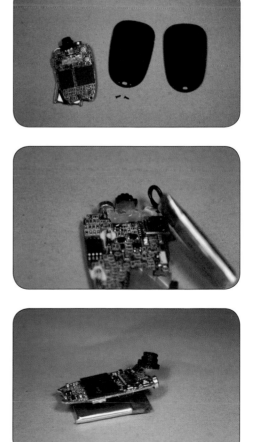

185

Step 4: Measuring for the Cuts

This will require some measuring and good judgment to get a good fit. We will be working with three pieces from the rocket kit in the next few steps. The nose cone is as it sounds: the wood nose of the rocket. The payload bay tube is the cardboard tube to contain the payload. The payload bay base is the wood piece that joins the payload bay to the body of the rocket. One end has a larger diameter than the other end.

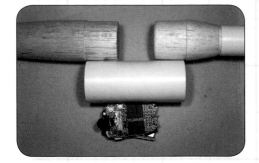

The wood nose cone and wood payload bay base take up a lot of space in the payload bay tube when everything is put together. This is not enough space for the camera to fit. We will cut some the wood from each piece to allow space for the camera inside the payload bay tube.

Mark the payload bay base and nose cone.

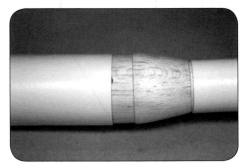

I placed the pieces together beside each other and positioned them as if they were assembled to get an idea of the space I need to clear. I placed the camera on top of the parts, about ½" from where the payload bay tube would rest on the payload bay base. Since the payload bay base will be glued securely into place, I decided to cut the most wood off of this piece. Using a pen, I marked a dot ½" from where the tube rests against the base. This means there will be ½" of wood left to secure the tube to the base. I then marked on the nose cone just above where the camera microphone is (silver cylinder) at approximately ¹¹/₁₆" from where the tube rests against the nose cone.

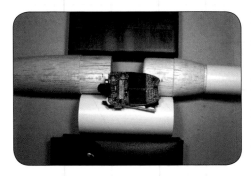

After sliding the payload tube down to the mark I made on the payload bay base, I then used the tube to draw a line all the way around the wood to use as a cutting guide.

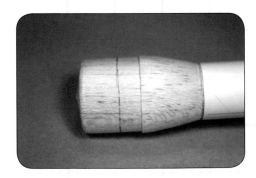

Step 5: Modifying the Payload Bay Base

Cut the payload bay base. The wood is soft Balsa, so it should cut easily with most saws. Just be careful not to apply a lot of pressure when holding or cutting, as you can compress or dent the wood. Hold the wood on the side of the line with the most wood. Place the saw blade on the line and pull towards yourself to get a groove started. Do not apply much pressure into the cut; the weight of the saw should be enough to cut the wood.

Using your guide line to keep your cut level, continue to saw through the wood. Rotate the base around so you cut around the outside first and keep your eye on the guide line to maintain your straight line. Continue cutting evenly all around towards the center. When you are almost done, cut through the center.

You will probably want to give your newly cut base a sanding to smooth it down, make it level, and remove any loose wood bits.

Step 6: Modifying the Nose Cone

The nose cone must be removable to place the camera inside each time you use it. It cannot be glued and must rely on friction to stay sealed during flight. This is why we will leave more wood on the nose cone after we cut it for the inside of the payload bay tube.

Use the same technique that was used on the payload base to draw a line around the nose cone wood where the measurement mark was made. Then, use the same technique as before to saw the nose cone. Sand the nose cone's cut surface

At this point, we should have enough space inside the payload bay to fit the camera. Place the payload base inside the payload tube. Place the camera inside the bay with the camera side at the top. Place the nose cone inside the payload tube. The base and the nose cone should slide in as far as they can, without being obstructed by the camera. You may need to make sure the lens is not blocking the nose cone and is positioned beside the camera circuit board in the tube. If there is not enough room, make note of how far the *nose cone* sticks out, and cut or sand off that length of wood from the nose cone.

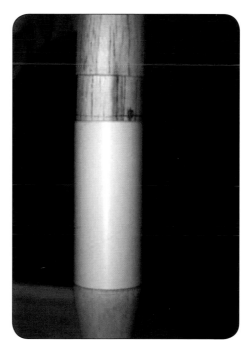

187

Step 7: Cut Hole for Camera Lens

The payload bay on the Estes Reflector is not transparent, so a hole must be cut in the side for the lens to poke through. Even if the payload bay tube was transparent, it would be wise to cut a hole for the lens to eliminate any distortion or other issues. This hole also serves to hold the camera steady during flight.

With the payload base inserted in the payload bay tube, gauge where the lens hole should go.

A couple of things to keep in mind for the hole placement:

- Once the lens is in the hole, the lens/ sensor cannot contact the nose cone. Make sure the hole is low enough for the nose cone to be fully inserted once the lens is in place.
- The hole must also be within reach of the lens ribbon cable. Placing the hole too low will put the hole out of reach of the short ribbon cable.

Using a pen or pencil, place a dot where the center of the lens hole should be on the outside of the tube. The center of my hole was marked at 1 ³⁄₁₆" from the top of the tube but may vary depending on where your payload base was cut. Take the camera out of the tube. Place the lens on the dot and center it on the dot. Using the pen, trace around the lens to create a circle in the shape of the lens.

If you have a Dremel, use a cone or parabolic shaped grinding stone to grind/sand a hole using the dot as a starting point. Use the circle as a guide to keep the hole centered. If you do not have a Dremel, use an X-acto knife to cut out the hole *within* the lens outline you traced. Push the spinning grinder into the tube to expand the hole until you near the size of the circular outline that was traced. The final diameter is approximately ¼". When the size of the

hole approaches the outline you traced, check to see if the lens can be pushed through the hole. The goal is for the lens to pass easily through the hole, without being so loose that the lens vibrates or too tight that it won't enter easily. Use an X-acto knife to clean up any loose cardboard left behind on the opening from the grinding process.

Check the final fit. Place the payload bay base into the tube, place the camera in the tube, maneuver the camera lens into the hole so it protrudes slightly from the tube, and place the nose cone on. Make any necessary adjustments for fit.

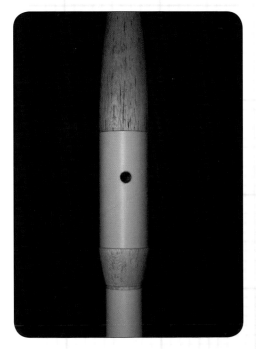

is achieved. This is important because, once the rocket is launched and the parachute is deployed, the nose cone will be pointing *down* and it will be the only thing holding the camera in the payload bay! The nose cone should fit tightly, yet it must still be removable by hand without damaging the rocket.

Step 9: Finish Building Your Rocket

Now that the payload bay is modified to carry the camera, finish any remaining steps for building your rocket, such as:

- Putting the eye screw into the payload bay base
- Attaching shock cord and parachute to eye screw
- Paint

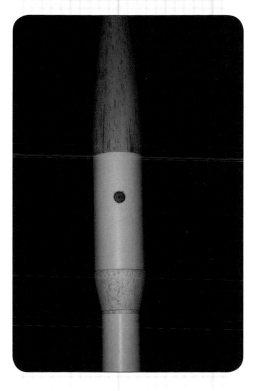

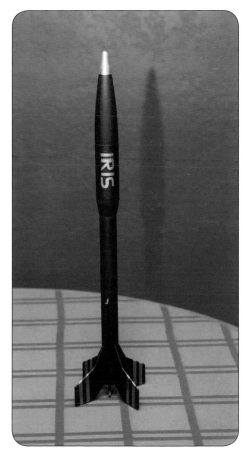

Step 8: Finish Payload Bay

Glue the payload bay base into the payload tube——glue it well. We have removed a lot of the wood and it will need a secure bond. Make sure the base is glued into the correct end of the payload tube, since the hole for the lens will not be centered along the length of the tube!

Make sure the nose cone has a very snug fit in the payload tube but is still removable. If necessary, wrap the wood section that is inserted into the payload tube with masking tape until a good fit

special

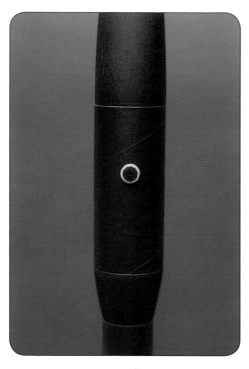

Step 10: Prepping Camera for Launch

Fully charge the camera battery. Insert Micro SD card into your camera Test your camera to make sure it works and view the test videos on a computer. Familiarize yourself with the buttons and function indicator lights. You'll want to practice inserting the camera into the rocket before launch day. It can be tricky and you'll be recording video the whole time you install the camera when you film a launch.

Perform all prep on the rocket necessary for launch (recovery wadding, load parachute, load engine, insert igniter, etc.). Turn on camera. Start the recording. Place the camera inside the payload bay tube. Maneuver the lens to point through the lens hole of the payload bay tube. While the lens is in place, tightly compress one ear plug, as you would when inserting it into your ear, and insert it vertically between the payload bay tube wall and the camera circuit board on the side of the circuit board away from the camera lens. Let it expand. Compress one more ear plug and insert it vertically as best you can between back of camera lens/sensor and camera circuit board. Let it expand. Use more earplugs if needed to hold the camera lens and circuit board in place. Once camera is secured with ear plugs, insert the nose cone into payload bay tube. You are recording and ready for launch!

Step 11: Post Launch

After your launch, recover the rocket and remove the camera. Stop the recording and turn it off. Set up the rocket and camera again for another launch if you'd like.

Editing

Now that you've launched your rocket and recorded video, you'll want to make your results presentable. As you will notice once you view your videos on a computer, the launch part of the video appears up-side down, while the video after parachute deployment is right side up. This is due to the different orientation of the camera and the payload bay during lift off and after parachute deployment. There is also a lot of unnecessary footage that was recorded during camera loading and unloading from the payload bay.

Simple and free video editing software such as Windows Movie Maker (what I used) can fix this video orientation issue, will allow editing, and are fairly easy to learn. With software like this, you can split your video into two sections and rotate the section that appears up-side down. If done properly, it gives the illusion that the camera was right side up the entire time! Nobody will know the difference and anyone who is familiar with rockets might scratch their heads wondering how you did it.

Nyan Cat Rocket
By: Deadendshop34
(http://www.instructables.com/
id/Nyan-Cat-Rocket/)

K9 has been bothering me for someone to hang out with while I'm in class, but my budget for this month is on the brink of falling into the Red. So I needed to come up with a buddy for K9 on the cheap. I started thinking about what I should make when I heard it coming from my roommate's room ("it" being the Nyan Cat theme). It clicked. I'm going to make a Nyan Cat for K9; I know cats and dog aren't typically the best of friends, but who can say no to a pop tart cat. My challenge this time is that Nyan cat loves to fly, so instead of being ground based, she needed to be air borne. With that in mind, I turned to rockets. I mean, after all, her natural habitat is space so it was a no brainier.

Step 1: Lanchpad

WARNING: This compressed air and PVC build can be dangerous. Check to see how much PSI your pipe can take and don't get anywhere near that number, because if the pipe breaks apart and flies everywhere, it could cut you like a knife.

Rockets with any type of combustibles would be a no-no in the dorm, so I went with the more dorm friendly compressed air. I also decided to make this at home; that way, I could test it out in the field and, if all went well, Nyan cat would come back with me.

Materials Needed for Lanchpad
- ½" PVC pipe—17 should be plenty with some left over.
- 4 bolts
- 1 inch coupling
- T PVC fitting
- 90° bend fitting
- PVC cap
- O-Ring
- PVC cement
- Soda bottle
- Wire firing pin
- Black and Decker workmate
- Air compressor
- Quick coupling for the air compressor going into the pipe and connecting to the air hose
- In my case, wasp spray—During testing, I got stung eleven times by yellow jackets in the ground.

As you can see from the photos, the PVC pipe was cut into sections and made a "T" shape using the two fittings and PVC cement mentioned above. Cap one end and add the quick coupling for the air compresser on the other end. Put an empty soda bottle on the pipe that is up on the 90° angle and mark it, because you're going to need to make a grove where you can slip the o-ring around. Next, drill two holes in the 1" coupling where the wire firing pin is and hold the top lip of the bottle. Once

special

192

that is done, drill out four holes on the bottom of the same coupling for the bolts. If you're lost, take a look at the pictures for additional help. Attach a rope or string to the firing pin.

The workmate will be used to stabilize the launch pad and add weight so it won't tip over.

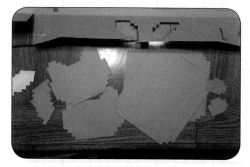

Step 2: Nyan Cat

You're going to need light weight material for the body. I used a very light weight cardboard. Design your cat however you want and print out a template. Now your cat can be any size you want as long as you size the printing to the length and width you want. I used the resin technique that they use on making halo costumes, only I didn't add any fiber glass.

After you get your cat cut out, put each separate part together, and applied, dried, and sanded the resin, then you can glue it all together. Once that is done, it's time to sand it and apply the cat look.

When putting together the body, measure your soda bottle width. That way, Nyan will go around the bottle, like a sock.*

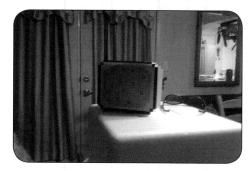

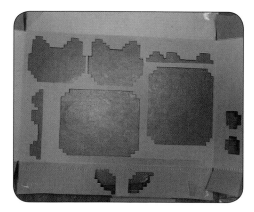

Step 3: 3 . . . 2 . . . 1 . . . Nyan!

Add streamers to Nyan for the rainbow trail. Next, secure the bottle to the launch tube and put in the firing pin. Now, slip on Nyan over the bottle and turn on your air compressor to a safe PSI; 50-85 will launch it a pretty good distance. Once your rocket is "Hot," give the countdown, step back, and pull the string attached to the firing pin. Enjoy Nyan blasting off into space with a rainbow trail.

The Black and Decker workmate is acting as a weight so the rocket doesn't fall over and shoot off towards you.

Rocket-Powered Matchbox Cars – Extreme!

By: Kipkay
(http://www.instructables.com/id/New-Rocket-Powered-Matchbox-Cars!---Extreme!/)

First of all, my inspiration for this project came from zjharva. This is a new version of Rocket-Powered Matchbox cars. Now you see what they really do on rocket power! I used Hot Wheels cars, but I felt they really needed to be called Matchbox because of what were about to do to them!

Step 1: What You Need

First of all, you will need a package of Estes A10-PT model rocket engines. You can find these at most Walmart stores, hobby shops, or other stores that carry model rockets.

Step 2: You Also Need

Something to attach the "engines" to the cars. I used 32-gauge wire that you can wrap around the vehicle and secure the engine safely during ignition.

Step 3: And . . .

You need something to guide the car on its track. Without this, the rocket shoots the car and rolls it, flipping and tumbling across the track. I used a coffee stirrer and, after cutting a small groove in the bottom of the car, cut it to size and glued it in place. This is the perfect diameter for the string that the car rides on.

Step 4: The Controller

I picked up an Estes Race Controller that runs on four AA batteries and has a long enough wire with alligator clips at the end. These will attach to the rocket igniters and fire the rocket!

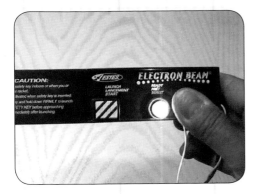

Step 5: Final Test Results!

This was wicked fun! We brought them to a tennis court, which was the perfect flat surface, and tested them out.

special

CONVERSION TABLES

One person's inch is another person's centimeter. Instructables projects come from all over the world, so here's a handy reference guide that will help keep your project on track.

Measurement								
	1 Millimeter	1 Centimeter	1 Meter	1 Inch	1 Foot	1 Yard	1 Mile	1 Kilometer
Millimeter	1	10	1,000	25.4	304.8	—	—	—
Centimeter	0.1	1	100	2.54	30.48	91.44	—	—
Meter	0.001	0.01	1	0.025	0.305	0.91	—	1,000
Inch	0.04	0.39	39.37	1	12	36	—	—
Foot	0.003	0.03	3.28	0.083	1	3	—	—
Yard	—	0.0109	1.09	0.28	033	1	—	—
Mile	—	—	—	—	—	—	1	0.62
Kilometer	—	—	1,000	—	—	—	1.609	1

Volume									
	1 Mil- liliter	1 Liter	1 Cubic Meter	1 Tea- spoon	1 Tablespoon	1 Fluid Ounce	1 Cup	1 Pint	1 Quart	1 Gal- lon
Milliliter	1	1,000	—	4.9	14.8	29.6	—	—	—	—
Liter	0.001	1	1,000	0.005	0.015	0.03	0.24	0.47	0.95	3.79
Cubic Meter	—	0.001	1	—	—	—	—	—	—	0.004
Teaspoon	0.2	202.9	—	1	3	6	48	—	—	—
Tablespoon	0.068	67.6	—	0.33	1	2	16	32	—	—
Fluid Ounce	0.034	33.8	—	0.167	0.5	1	8	16	32	—
Cup	0.004	4.23	—	0.02	0.0625	0.125	1	2	4	16
Pint	0.002	2.11	—	0.01	0.03	0.06	05	1	2	8
Quart	0.001	1.06	—	0.005	0.016	0.03	0.25	.05	1	4
Gallon	—	0.26	264.17	0.001	0.004	0.008	0.0625	0.125	0.25	1

conversion tables

Mass and Weight						
	1 Gram	1 Kilogram	1 Metric Ton	1 Ounce	1 Pound	1 Short Ton
Gram	1	1,000	—	28.35	—	—
Kilogram	0.001	1	1,000	0.028	0.454	—
Metric Ton	—	0.001	1	—	—	0.907
Ounce	0.035	35.27	—	1	16	—
Pound	0.002	2.2	—	0.0625	1	2,000
Short Ton	—	0.001	1.1	—	—	1

Speed		
	1 Mile per hour	1 Kilometer per hour
Miles per hour	1	0.62
Kilometers per hour	1.61	1

Temperature		
	Fahrenheit (°F)	Celsius (°C)
Fahrenheit	—	(°C x 1.8) + 32
Celsius	(°F − 32) / 1.8	—